Lecture Notes in Computer Science　　　13868

Founding Editors

Gerhard Goos
Juris Hartmanis

The series Lecture Notes in Computer Science (LNCS), including its subseries Lecture Notes in Artificial Intelligence (LNAI) and Lecture Notes in Bioinformatics (LNBI), has established itself as a medium for the publication of new developments in computer science and information technology research, teaching, and education.

LNCS enjoys close cooperation with the computer science R & D community, the series counts many renowned academics among its volume editors and paper authors, and collaborates with prestigious societies. Its mission is to serve this international community by providing an invaluable service, mainly focused on the publication of conference and workshop proceedings and postproceedings. LNCS commenced publication in 1973.

Stephen Chang

Editor

Trends in Functional Programming

24th International Symposium, TFP 2023
Boston, MA, USA, January 13–15, 2023
Revised Selected Papers

 Springer

Editor
Stephen Chang (ID)
University of Massachusetts Boston
Boston, MA, USA

ISSN 0302-9743   ISSN 1611-3349 (electronic)
Lecture Notes in Computer Science
ISBN 978-3-031-38937-5   ISBN 978-3-031-38938-2 (eBook)
https://doi.org/10.1007/978-3-031-38938-2

This Springer imprint is published by the registered company Springer Nature Switzerland AG
The registered company address is: Gewerbestrasse 11, 6330 Cham, Switzerland

Preface

This volume contains revised selected papers that were presented at the 24th International Symposium on Trends in Functional Programming (TFP 2023), which was held at the University of Massachusetts, Boston (UMass Boston) from January 13–15, 2023. The symposium was co-located with the 12th International Workshop on Trends in Functional Programming in Education (TFPIE 2023), which took place on January 12, 2023. Notably, this year marked a return to in-person symposium events, after the previous two events were held online.

TFP is an international forum for researchers with interests in all aspects of functional programming, taking a broad view of current and future trends in this area. It aspires to be a lively environment for presenting the latest research results and other contributions. Reviewing for TFP is a two-phase, single-blind process where authors may either submit a full paper for review before the symposium, or submit an extended abstract before the symposium, followed by a full paper afterwards that incorporates feedback from both the pre-symposium reviews and the presentations. Each paper receives at least three reviews in each round.

This year we received fourteen total submissions. Twelve were presented at the symposium, along with three keynote talks: Jay McCarthy, co-founder and CTO of Reach, Inc., presented "Reach: A Language for DApp Development"; Alley Stoughton, from Boston University, presented "Applying Cryptography's Real/Ideal Paradigm to PL Security"; and Norman Ramsey, from Tufts University, presented "A New Book on Programming Languages. Why?" After the post-symposium review phase, revised versions of six papers were selected for inclusion in these proceedings. The final selections spanned a wide variety of topics including DSL design and implementation, dependent type systems, instruction set architecture, data structures, and logic programming.

In addition, TFP offers two prizes: the John McCarthy award for the best paper and the David Turner award for the best student paper. The paper "MatchMaker: A DSL for Game-Theoretic Matching" by Prashant Kumar and Martin Erwig was awarded the best paper prize. The paper "Impredicative Encodings of Inductive-Inductive Data in Cedille" by Andrew Marmaduke, Larry Diehl, and Aaron Stump was awarded the best student paper prize.

All of this was only possible thanks to the hard work of the authors, the insightful contributions of the Program Committee members, and the thoughtful advice from the TFP steering committee. Further, UMass Boston not only hosted the event, but also provided financial and organizational support. In particular we would like to acknowledge Elif Gurel, Debbie Wade, and Karen Doherty for generously helping to organize all the events. We thank everyone profusely for making this year's symposium a success.

April 2023   Stephen Chang

Organization

Program Committee and General Chair

Stephen Chang   University of Massachusetts Boston, USA

Program Committee

Peter Achten	Radboud University, The Netherlands
Nada Amin	Harvard University, USA
Ambrose Bonnaire-Sergeant	Untypable LLC, USA
Laura M. Castro	University of A Coruña, Spain
John Clements	Cal Poly, USA
Youyou Cong	Tokyo Institute of Technology, Japan
Paul Downen	University of Massachusetts Lowell, USA
Kathy Gray	Meta Platforms, Inc., UK
Ben Greenman	University of Utah, USA
Jason Hemann	Seton Hall University, USA
Patricia Johann	Appalachian State University, USA
Alexis King	Tweag, USA
Julia Lawall	Inria-Paris, France
Daniel Patterson	Northeastern University, USA
Barak Pearlmutter	Maynooth University, Ireland
Norman Ramsey	Tufts University, USA
Ilya Sergey	National University of Singapore, Singapore
Melinda Tóth	Eötvös Loránd University, Hungary
Ningning Xie	University of Toronto, Canada

Sponsored by University of Massachusetts Boston

Contents

Impredicative Encodings
of Inductive-Inductive Data in Cedille

Andrew Marmaduke[(✉)], Larry Diehl, and Aaron Stump

The University of Iowa, Iowa City, IA, USA
{andrew.marmaduke,larry.diehl,aaron.stump}@uiowa.edu

Abstract. Cedille is a dependently typed programming language known for expressive and efficient impredicative encodings. In this work, we show that encodings of induction-induction are also possible by employing a standard technique from other encodings in Cedille, where a type representing the shape of data is intersected with a predicate that further constrains. Thus, just as with indexed inductive data, Cedille can encode a notion that is often axiomatically postulated or directly implemented in other dependent type theories without sacrificing efficiency.

Keywords: Impredicative Encoding · Induction-Induction · Cedille

1 Introduction

Induction-induction is an extension of mutual inductive datatypes that further empowers a user to specify exactly the associated inhabitants. Denoted correct-by-construction, constructors are specified so that only the data of interest are expressible which prevents error handling or other boilerplate code for so-called "junk" data. These kinds of definitions were explored in detail by Forsberg et al. [3,11,12,22]. Mutual inductive datatypes in their simplest incarnation define two datatypes whose constructors may refer to the type of the other. The canonical example is the indexed datatypes Even and Odd.

$$\text{data Even} : \mathbb{N} \to \star \text{ where}$$
$$\text{ezer} : \text{Even } 0$$
$$\text{esuc} : (n : \mathbb{N}) \to \text{Odd } n \to \text{Even (suc } n)$$
$$\text{data Odd} : \mathbb{N} \to \star \text{ where}$$
$$\text{osuc} : (n : \mathbb{N}) \to \text{Even } n \to \text{Odd (suc } n)$$

Induction-induction expands on this by allowing a type to be the *index* of the other. Thus, instead of two mutually defined types $A, B : \star$ there are two types $A : \star$ and $B : A \to \star$ mutually defined. Of course, the types can refer to one another in their constructors as before. The canonical example of induction-induction is a type representing the syntax of a dependent type theory. The Ctx and Ty types (excluding a type representing terms) are defined:

S. Chang (Ed.): TFP 2023, LNCS 13868, pp. 1–15, 2023.
https://doi.org/10.1007/978-3-031-38938-2_1

```
data Ctx : ⋆ where
  nil : Ctx
  cons : (Γ : Ctx) → Ty Γ → Ctx
data Ty : Ctx → ⋆ where
  base : (Γ : Ctx) → Ty Γ
  arrow : (Γ : Ctx) → (A : Ty Γ) → (B : Ty (cons Γ A)) → Ty Γ
```

Induction-induction is of particular interest when modeling programming language syntax. Indeed, a more general formulation of quotient inductive-inductive datatypes was shown to model dependent type theories with induction principles modulo definitional equality [2]. From the perspective of constructing Domain Specific Languages (DSLs) induction-induction is a desirable technique if available.

DSLs are not the only interesting data that can be modelled with induction-induction. A type A and a predicate $P : A \to \star$ may be mutually defined by induction-induction to enforce some desired property on the data of A. For example, a ListSet of natural numbers where all elements must be unique:

```
data ListSet : ⋆ where
  nil : ListSet
  cons : (n : ℕ) → (ℓ : ListSet) → Unique n ℓ → ListSet
data Unique : ℕ → ListSet → ⋆ where
  triv : (n : ℕ) → Unique n nil
  ucons : (n m : ℕ) → (ℓ : ListSet)
          → m ≠ n → Unique m ℓ → Unique m (cons n ℓ)
```

While such a type can be defined via other methods (e.g. using quotients [20]), it is sometimes easier or more natural to define the property inductively. Additionally, the initial data without the constraining predicate may have no other use, thus a stronger guarantee is conveyed by demanding the data adheres to some predicate in its definition. Finally, there are some constructions in mathematical practice that have natural definitions via induction-induction in dependent type theory such as Conway's Surreal Numbers [22].

This paper reports a novel result that induction-induction is a *derivable* concept within the dependently typed programming language Cedille. Additionally, a generic encoding of induction-induction is formalized in the Cedille tool [formalization]. In fact, all notions of data are derived by other type constructors in Cedille with induction-induction being the latest example. While other dependent type theories support induction-induction they do so by extending the core theory of datatypes. This is a valid approach, but it is the philosophy of Cedille that a smaller trusted computing base (i.e. a small core type checker) is a more desirable feature when designing a tool for dependent type theories. Moreover, other tools (as of 2022, Coq is one such example) do not permit inductive-inductive datatypes.

2 Background on Cedille

Cedille is a dependently typed programming language with a type theory based on the Calculus of Constructions (CC) with three extensions: erased functions, dependent intersections, and equality [25,26]. Many interesting encodings are possible with this theory including inductive data and simulated large eliminations [9,15].

2.1 Erased Functions and Erasure

$$\frac{\Gamma, x : T \vdash t' : T' \quad x \notin FV(|t'|)}{\Gamma \vdash \Lambda x{:}T.\, t' : \forall x{:}T.\, T'} \qquad \frac{\Gamma \vdash t : \forall x{:}T'.\, T \quad \Gamma \vdash t' : T'}{\Gamma \vdash t \text{ -}t' : [t'/x]T}$$

$$|\Lambda x{:}T.\, t| \;=\; |t| \qquad\qquad |t \text{ -}t'| \;=\; |t|$$

Fig. 1. Erased Functions.

Erased functions as shown in Fig. 1 represent function spaces where the variable may not appear free in the erasure of the body. This type former is inspired by the implicit functions of Miquel [21]. The erasure of a term, $|t|$, is defined with each corresponding extension. Additionally, the definitional equality of the theory is extended to mean $|t_1| \equiv_{\beta\eta} |t_2|$ i.e. that two terms are definitionally equal if the $\beta\eta$-normal forms of their erasures are equivalent up-to renaming. We take the liberty of a syntax style resembling Agda and use $(x : T_1) \Rightarrow T_2$ to be an equivalent syntax for $\forall x{:}T_1.\, T_2$. Note that types in Cedille are always erased at the term level.

Erased functions allow for a fine-grained control over the relevant shape of a term which is critical when intersecting. Moreover, indices are almost always conceptually viewed as erased, but this fact is not usually expressible in a type theory. With erased functions, indices can always be marked as erased. Note that erased functions are not like implicit arguments in other languages where a term is inferred via unification. Instead, an erased function is closer to the erased functions of Quantitative Type Theory (QTT) [4].

For example, a constructor for a vector type would have both its type parameter and its natural number index erased:

$$\text{vcons} : (A : \star) \Rightarrow (n : \mathbb{N}) \Rightarrow A \to \text{Vec } A\ n \to \text{Vec } A\ (\text{succ } n)$$

Then the erasure of a value of type Vec forgets the index arguments of constructors, e.g.

$$|\text{vcons -}\mathbb{N}\text{ -}1\ t\ (\text{vnil -}\mathbb{N})| = |\text{vcons}|\ |t|\ |\text{vnil}|$$

As a consequence, it is possible to define a List type such that $|\text{cons}| = |\text{vcons}|$ and $|\text{nil}| = |\text{vnil}|$. While erased functions can be expressed in a QTT style the critical feature, i.e. the interaction with definitional equality, is orthogonal to usage restrictions on variables.

2.2 Dependent Intersections

$$\frac{\Gamma \vdash t_1 : T_1 \quad \Gamma \vdash t_2 : [t_1/x]T_2 \quad |t_1| = |t_2|}{\Gamma \vdash [t_1, t_2] : \iota\, x : T_1 . T_2}$$

$$\frac{\Gamma \vdash t : \iota\, x : T_1 . T_2}{\Gamma \vdash t.1 : T_1} \qquad \frac{\Gamma \vdash t : \iota\, x : T_1 . T_2}{\Gamma \vdash t.2 : [t.1/x]T_2}$$

$$|[t_1, t_2]| = |t_1| \qquad |t.1| = |t| \qquad |t.2| = |t|$$

Fig. 2. Dependent Intersection.

Inspired by Kopylov [19], dependent intersections, as shown in Fig. 2, can be interpreted intuitively as a kind of refinement type. While the namesake makes sense, because the terms of an intersection must be definitionally equal, the usage we are primarily interested in is to constrain some type via a predicate that matches its shape. Note, this is a critical and powerful application which obviates many other concerns with refinement types. Again, a syntax style resembling Agda is used with $(x : T_1) \cap T_2$ being equivalent syntax for $\iota\, x : T_1 . T_2$. While useful for presentation, these alternative syntaxes are not possible in the Cedille tool, thus an inspection of the formalization will require understanding the original syntactic forms.

2.3 Equality

The propositional equality of Cedille, as shown in Fig. 3, is necessary for reasoning about the shape of terms and finalizing the development of an induction principle for the various possible encodings in Cedille. Cedille's equality is different from other dependent type theories like Agda. Indeed, it is irrelevant, not inductive, and works over *untyped* terms. Equality is necessary to complete derivations of induction and for instantiation of non-trivial casts.

Instead of an inductive eliminator like the J axiom of Martin-Löf's Identity Type Cedille's equality has a rewrite rule. The ρ rule requires an equation as evidence and introduces a binder to select the location where rewrites are performed. For example, given $e : \{x \simeq y\}$ and the goal type $P\,(x + x)$ a rewrite is performed on the *first* x via $\rho\, e\, @\, i.\, P\,(i + x) - t$ where $t : P\,(y + x)$. Rewriting is *irrelevant* because the rewrite machinery is completely erased, meaning definitional equality between terms does not depend on rewrites.

Additionally, Cedille's equality type has another elimination form inspired by the direct computation rule of Nuprl, φ [1]. The φ rule allows a term's type to be changed to the type of any other term that it is definitionally equal to. Recall that definitional equality is up-to erasure, thus given $e : \{\text{cons} \simeq \text{vcons}\}$ the following term is well-formed: $\varphi\, e - \text{cons}\, \{\text{vcons}\}$. This changes the type of vcons to the type of cons. Note that these kinds of casts between types would

$$\frac{FV(t) \subseteq dom(\Gamma)}{\Gamma \vdash \beta : \{t \simeq t\}} \quad \frac{\Gamma \vdash t : \{t_1 \simeq t_2\} \quad \Gamma \vdash t' : [t_2/x]T}{\Gamma \vdash \rho\, t\, @\, x.T - t' : [t_1/x]T}$$

$$\frac{\Gamma \vdash t : \{t_1 \simeq t_2\} \quad \Gamma \vdash t_1 : T}{\Gamma \vdash \varphi\, t - t_1\, \{t_2\} : T} \quad \frac{\Gamma \vdash t : \{\lambda x.\lambda y.\, x \simeq \lambda x.\lambda y.\, y\}}{\Gamma \vdash \delta - t : T}$$

$$|\beta| = \lambda x.\, x \quad |\rho\, t\, @\, x.T - t'| = |t'|$$

$$|\varphi\, t - t_1\, \{t_2\}| = |t_2| \quad |\delta - t| = \lambda x.\, x$$

Fig. 3. Equality.

not be possible if equality were over typed terms. The φ rule, like the ρ rule, is irrelevant.

Finally, the δ rule enables proving inequalities between terms. In particular, the δ rule asserts that there is *at least two* distinct terms in the equational theory. However, this is enough to prove the inequality of several terms by constructing functions to disambiguate them. Surprisingly, the δ rule is critical to constructing simulated large eliminations [15].

2.4 Casts

A *cast* is a derived construct in Cedille that encodes an identity function between two, potentially definitionally distinct, types. Figure 4 presents a rule-based description of casts. Note that there are trivial casts from a dependent intersection to its first or second component. The φ constructor of the equality type is responsible for creating more interesting inhabitants of the Cast type. Casts are introduced using φ in the following way:

$$\text{intrCast } -f\ -t = [\lambda x.\, \varphi\ (t\ x) - (f\ x)\ \{x\},\ \beta]$$

They are eliminated by φ and projection:

$$\text{cast } -t = \varphi\ t.2 - t.1\ \{\lambda x.\, x\}$$

Casts are critical to deriving efficient inductive data. By *efficient,* we mean that the production of subdata is emulated with a constant number of β-reductions, and that folds over data is emulated in a proportional number of β-reductions relative to the size of the data. For example, the predecessor function for unary Natural numbers should be $\mathcal{O}(1)$ reductions and addition should be $\mathcal{O}(n)$ reductions in the first argument.

Efficiency is an important aspect of lambda encodings of inductive data as early on it was shown that Church encoded data requires linear time to construct predecessors [24]. Parigot proposed an encoding with constant time predecessors but at the cost of normal forms with exponential size [23]. Reasonable computational properties of lambda encodings were not extensively studied because

$$\frac{\Gamma \vdash f : S \to T \quad \Gamma \vdash t : \Pi\, x\!:\!S.\, \{f\, x \simeq x\}}{\Gamma \vdash \mathsf{intrCast} \text{ -}f \text{ -}t : \mathsf{Cast}\ S\ T}$$

$$\frac{\Gamma \vdash t : \mathsf{Cast}\ S\ T}{\Gamma \vdash \mathsf{cast} \text{ -}t : S \to T}$$

$$|\mathsf{intrCast} \text{ -}f \text{ -}t| = \lambda\, x.\, x \quad |\mathsf{cast} \text{ -}t| = \lambda\, x.\, x$$

Fig. 4. Casts.

the inability to derive inductive data was considered a non-starter [13]. However, the research direction of Cedille focused on demonstrating that inductive lambda encodings are a possibility, but without an efficient lambda encoding axiomatic definitions of inductive data are greatly preferred. Mendler-style data proved to be the ideal candidate for an efficient encoding with good space and time characteristics [10].

2.5 Indexed Inductive Data

Indexed-inductive datatypes are also a *derived* notion in Cedille. The Cedille tool supports special syntax with motive inference and other quality of life improvements to ease working with data. A complete derivation of indexed-inductive data is provided in the formalization [encoding]. Additionally, all formalized work presented in this paper uses this encoding. However, occasionally the convenient syntax is used instead, particularly when defining functors that are provided to generic encodings. This syntax allows the construction of data, e.g. of Natural numbers and Pairs:

$$\text{data Nat } : \star =$$
$$|\text{ zero : Nat}$$
$$|\text{ succ : Nat} \to \text{Nat}$$

$$\text{data Pair } (A : \star)\ (B : \star) : \star =$$
$$|\text{ pair} : A \to B \to \text{Pair}$$

and standard eliminators, e.g. pattern-matching elimination of pairs:

$$\text{fst} : (A : \star) \Rightarrow (B : \star) \Rightarrow \text{Pair } A\ B \to A$$
$$= \Lambda\ A.\ \Lambda\ B.\ \lambda\ p.\ \mu'\ p\ \{\ \text{pair } a\ b \to a\ \}$$

and recursion on natural numbers:

$$\text{add} : \text{Nat} \to \text{Nat} \to \text{Nat}$$
$$= \lambda\ n.\ \lambda\ m.\ \mu\ \text{rec.}\ m\ \{$$
$$|\ \text{zero} \to n$$
$$|\ \text{succ } m' \to \text{succ } (\text{rec } m')\ \}$$

The operational semantics of μ' is case-branch selection, so for example fst (pair zero (succ zero)) reduces to zero. The operational semantics of μ is combined case-branch selection and fixed-point unrolling. For example, for any m and n of type Nat, add (succ m) n reduces to

$$\text{succ } (\mu \text{ rec. } m \ \{ \text{ zero} \rightarrow n \mid \text{succ } m' \rightarrow \text{succ } (\text{rec } m') \ \})$$

Declared datatypes automatically come with induction principles. For example:

$$\text{addZeroRight} : (n : \text{Nat}) \rightarrow \{\text{add } n \text{ zero} \simeq n\}$$
$$= \lambda \ n. \ \mu \ ih. \ n \ @ \ \lambda \ x : \text{Nat.} \ \{\text{add } x \text{ zero} \simeq x \ \} \ \{$$
$$\mid \text{zero} \rightarrow \beta$$
$$\mid \text{succ } n' \rightarrow \rho \ (ih \ n') \ @ \ y. \ \{\text{succ } y \simeq \text{succ } n'\} - \beta \ \}$$

A guiding motive (the type after the first @) is given explicitly to the μ construct to help guide typing of each case-branch. Further discussion of the core ideas will not use the μ syntax and instead will take an informal approach, but this syntax is necessary for understanding the formalization.

3   Induction-Induction Encoding

3.1   The Core Idea

Impredicative encodings of inductive data follow from the observation that a simple view of the type in terms of System F and an induction principle stated relative to this simpler view yields the full inductive type when intersected. For example, consider a Church encoded Natural number where we first define the standard impredicative encoding in System F.

$$\text{CNat} = (X : \star) \Rightarrow X \rightarrow (X \rightarrow X) \rightarrow X$$

Then, the inductive predicate we expect of natural numbers but stated relative to CNats:

$$\text{CNatInd} = \lambda \ n. \ (P : \text{CNat} \rightarrow \star) \Rightarrow P \text{ czero}$$
$$\rightarrow ((x : \text{CNat}) \Rightarrow P \ x \rightarrow P \ (\text{csucc } x)) \rightarrow P \ n$$

Note that, critically, the subdata in the successor case of the induction predicative is quantified with an erased arrow. This allows the computational content of both CNat and CNatInd to match while simultaneously allowing for the expected induction principle to be stated. Now, the full inductive type is the intersection,

$$\text{Nat} = (x : \text{CNat}) \cap \text{CNatInd } x$$

where the correct induction principle in terms of Nat is derivable.

The same core idea works for reducing inductive-inductive data to indexed inductive data. For example, Ctx and Ty are encoded first by defining a mutual inductive type representing their shapes:

$$\text{data Pre} : \mathbb{B} \to \star \text{ where}$$
$$\text{pnil} : \text{Pre tt}$$
$$\text{pcons} : \text{Pre tt} \to \text{Pre ff} \to \text{Pre tt}$$
$$\text{pbase} : \text{Pre tt} \to \text{Pre ff}$$
$$\text{parrow} : \text{Pre tt} \to \text{Pre ff} \to \text{Pre ff} \to \text{Pre ff}$$

Now Pre tt is the PreCtx and Pre ff is the PreTy, the initial shapes of both types. Second, we construct a predicate over Pre types capturing induction relative to a Pre value.

$$\text{data Ind} : (b : \mathbb{B}) \to \text{elim } b \to \star \text{ where}$$
$$\text{gnil} : \text{Ind tt (in}_1 \text{ pnil)}$$
$$\text{gcons} : (c : \text{PreCtx}) \Rightarrow \text{Ind tt (in}_1 c)$$
$$\to (t : \text{PreTy}) \Rightarrow \text{Ind ff (in}_2 c \, t)$$
$$\to \text{Ind tt (in}_1 (\text{pcons } c \, t))$$
$$\text{gbase} : (c : \text{PreCtx}) \Rightarrow \text{Ind tt (in}_1 c) \to \text{Ind ff (in}_2 (\text{pbase } c))$$
$$\text{garrow} : (c : \text{PreCtx}) \Rightarrow \text{Ind tt (in}_1 c)$$
$$\to (a : \text{PreTy}) \Rightarrow \text{Ind ff (in}_2 c \, a)$$
$$\to (b : \text{PreTy}) \Rightarrow \text{Ind ff (in}_2 (\text{pcons } c \, a) \, b)$$
$$\to \text{Ind ff (in}_2 c \, (\text{parrow } c \, a \, b))$$

where elim b is a simulated large elimination [15] with constructors

$$\text{in}_1 : \text{Pre tt} \to \text{elim tt}$$
$$\text{in}_2 : \text{Pre tt} \to \text{Pre ff} \to \text{elim ff}$$

Notice that the type Ind, when erased arrows and the elim b dependencies are removed, is *exactly* the Pre type. Moreover, in Cedille when two inductive types are defined with the same number of constructors, as long as the relevant types of those constructors agree, then the constructors themselves are equal. Thus, we have that pnil is definitionally equal to gnil, and likewise for the three remaining constructors. Conceptually, we will see that we can also view Ind as capturing the canonical (or normal) elements of Pre that are inductive.

Now, the complete inductive-inductive types may be defined by the intersections:

$$\text{Ctx} = (x : \text{PreCtx}) \cap \text{Ind tt (in}_1 x)$$
$$\text{Ty} = \lambda \, c : \text{Ctx}. \, (x : \text{PreTy}) \cap \text{Ind ff (in}_2 c.1 \, x)$$

Again, the expected induction principles are derivable in terms of Ctx and Ty. Note that the technique of encoding mutual inductive types via indexed inductive types is a standard trick [18]. Moreover, the efficiency of the encoding is dependent entirely on the efficiency of the underlying indexed inductive data encoding.

3.2 Generic Encoding: First Variant

To obtain a generic version of the core idea we first must describe a functor representation of the required data. First, the ShapeF functor must encode the shape of all possible constructors. Let n be the number of datatypes under definition, then

$$(\text{Fin } n \to \star) \to \text{Fin } n \to \star$$

is the type of the ShapeF functor. Of course, in order for this to really be a functor it must be monotonic. A functor F with index I is *monotonic* if it preserves casts on indexed data, or concretely if it satisfies the following property:

$$(A : I \to \star) \to (B : I \to \star)$$
$$\to ((i : I) \to \text{Cast } (A\ i)\ (B\ i))$$
$$\to (i : I) \to \text{Cast } (F\ A\ i)\ (F\ B\ i)$$

Second, we must constrain the shape with a NormalF functor. Let Shape be the inductive type corresponding to a monotonic ShapeF functor. Let Idx be the type $(i : \text{Fin } n) \times (\text{Tuple } n \text{ Shape (fsucc } -n\ i))$ where $(a : A) \times P\ a$ is a derived sigma type and Tuple n Shape (fsucc $-n\ i$) is a derived simulated large elimination with the computation rules:

tupleP : Tuple n Shape (fsucc $-n\ i$) $\to$ (Shape i) $\times$ (Tuple n Shape i)

tupleS : (Shape i) $\times$ (Tuple n Shape i) $\to$ Tuple n Shape (fsucc $-n\ i$)

tupleZ : Tuple n Shape 0 $\to$ Unit

The formalization of Tuple is available in [lib/tuple.ced]. Now, the type of NormalF is

$$\text{NormalF} : (\text{Idx} \to \star) \to \text{Idx} \to \star$$

and it must additionally be monotonic relative to Idx.

Finally, we must know that the computational shape of NormalF data is the same as ShapeF data. That is, we require a cast:

$$(i : \text{Idx}) \to \text{Cast (NormalF } i)\ (\text{ShapeF (fst } i))$$

With all of this input data supplied the core idea may be carried out. Let QIdx be the type $(i : \text{Fin } n) \times (\text{Tuple } n \text{ Shape } i)$, Shape be the inductive type constructed from ShapeF, and Normal the inductive type constructed from NormalF. Then the *quotient* is

$$\text{Quotient } i = (s : \text{Shape}) \cap (\text{Normal (pair (fst } i)\ (\text{tupleS (pair } s\ i))))$$

Notice that QIdx contains the indexes of all previously defined types in the chain, i.e. the types with fewer indices. The final Shape missing from QIdx is the very Shape to be constrained by the corresponding Normal. We have called this type a quotient because this construction, upon further reflection, is a generic quotient construction. The complete formalization of this encoding is available in [indind.ced]. However, it has two flaws:

1. the input data is onerous, requiring specifying the constructors twice and proving an unnecessary cast;
2. and the indices of Quotient are Shapes instead of Quotients.

As seen in Sect. 3.1 for specific datatypes the second criticism is fixable. Indeed, if we want to elaborate a custom syntactic representation of induction-induction to this encoding then these problems are both recoverable, but implementing this custom syntax is time-consuming. Moreover, Cedille's theory has a wealth of potential inductive encodings whose limits are not yet realized. Instead, we discuss a way of fixing the above hiccups internally.

3.3   Generic Encoding: Second Variant

Luckily, we do not need to start over. We define a smaller set of inputs and use those inputs to construct the necessary data for the quotient construction. Then, using the resulting types and induction principles from the quotient encoding, build the expected types and induction principles for the smaller input.

For this variant we focus on constructing only two types as opposed to any arbitrary n types. Consider a functor

$$F : (X : \star) \to (Y : X \to \star) \to \star$$

where X is conceptually the abstract representation of the first inductive type and Y is the abstract representation of the second inductive type. Then, a functor for the second type

$$G : (X : \star) \to (Y : X \to \star) \to (alg : F\ X\ Y \to X) \to X \to \star$$

has almost the same signature but crucially must be given an algebra to construct abstract Xs from $F\ X\ Y$ data. For example, CtxF and TyF functors are defined in this style as:

> data CtxF $(X : \star)\ (Y : X \to \star)$: $\star$ where
>   nilF : CtxF
>   consF : $(g : X) \to Y\ g \to$ CtxF

> data TyF $(X : \star)\ (Y : X \to \star)\ (alg : \text{CtxF}\ X\ Y \to X)$: $X \to \star$ where
>   baseF : $(g : X) \to$ TyF g
>   arrowF : $(g : X) \to (a : Y\ g) \to (b : Y\ (alg\ (\text{consF}\ g\ a))) \to$ TyF g

Note that the arrowF constructor is only possible with the additional *alg* parameter. These new functors require their own conditions of monotonicity, but the core idea is the same: the functor must preserve casts. In order to specify this requirement for the G functor there must be two algebras. However, the algebras should both correspond to the constructor for CtxF! Therefore, the additional restraint is imposed that the algebras are definitionally equal. The formalized monotonicity conditions are available in [indind2/mono.ced]. The two functors, F and G, with proofs that they are monotonic is all that is needed to derive the corresponding inductive types.

With this input data we proceed by defining a ShapeF and NormalF to instantiate the quotient encoding. To define ShapeF, let R : Fin 2 → ⋆ be the abstract type, then we have two constructors:

$$\text{ShapeFinF} : F \ (R \ 0) \ (\lambda \_. \ R \ 1) \to \text{ShapeF} \ 0$$

$$\text{ShapeFinG} : \forall \ A \ mA \ inj \Rightarrow (r : \text{IndA} \ 0) \Rightarrow$$
$$G \ (\text{IndA} \ 0) \ (\lambda \ i. \ \text{inA} \ (inj \ i)) \ r$$
$$\to \text{ShapeF} \ 1$$

Note a peculiarity in the definition of ShapeFinG. We must postulate a functor A of the same type as ShapeF that is monotonic (mA) and has an injection (inj). With this data, an inductive type (IndA) is instantiated with a corresponding constructor (inA). This abstracts the inductive type Shape that can not yet be spoken about, but is otherwise needed to enable typing G data. Proving monotonicity for this functor is straightforward. The full formalization is available in [indind2/shape.ced].

Next we define NormalF, recall that the index is defined in terms of Tuple, although the size of the Tuple is restricted to two types. To simplify the presentation we assume the functions

$$\text{in}_1 : \text{Shape} \ 0 \to \text{Idx}$$

and

$$\text{in}_2 : \text{Shape} \ 1 \to \text{Shape} \ 0 \to \text{Idx}$$

have been defined. Also, we elide casts to reduce the noise in the presentation. Let R : Idx → ⋆ be the abstract type.

$$\text{let } A \ 0 = (s : \text{Shape} \ 0) \cap R \ (\text{in}_1 \ c)$$
$$\text{let } A \ 1 = \lambda \ x : A \ 0. \ (s : \text{Shape} \ 1) \cap R \ (\text{in}_2 \ s \ x.1)$$
$$\text{NormalFinF} : (xs : F \ (A \ 0) \ (A \ 1))$$
$$\text{NormalF} \ (\text{in}_1 \ (\text{inShape -0} \ (\text{ShapeFinF} \ xs)))$$

The constructor NormalFinG follows the same pattern as ShapeFinG by abstracting an arbitrary functor A that stands in for a Normal as opposed to a Shape. The only additional requirement is that the inductive type IndA must be castable to the abstract type R. We elide its concrete definition because it is technical but not conceptually harder than ShapeFinG. The full formalization is available in [indind2/constraint.ced].

The definitions are carefully chosen so that a NormalF casts into a ShapeF for compatible indices which completes all required input to instantiate the quotient generic encoding. Now, after instantiation, the types TypeF : $\star$ and TypeG : TypeF $\rightarrow \star$ are definable. Notice that TypeG has the correct index. Moreover, the constructors:

$$\text{inF} : F \text{ TypeF TypeG} \rightarrow \text{TypeF}$$

$$\text{inG} : (i : \text{TypeF}) \Rightarrow G \text{ TypeF TypeG inF } i \rightarrow \text{TypeG } i$$

and the associated induction principles:

$$\text{inductF} : (P : \text{TypeF} \rightarrow \star) \rightarrow (Q : (i : \text{TypeF}) \rightarrow \text{TypeG } i \rightarrow \star)$$
$$\rightarrow \text{PrfAlgF } P \ Q \rightarrow \text{PrfAlgG } P \ Q \rightarrow (x : \text{TypeF}) \rightarrow P \ x$$

$$\text{inductG} : (P : \text{TypeF} \rightarrow \star) \rightarrow (Q : (i : \text{TypeF}) \rightarrow \text{TypeG } i \rightarrow \star)$$
$$\rightarrow \text{PrfAlgF } P \ Q \rightarrow \text{PrfAlgG } P \ Q \rightarrow (i : \text{TypeF}) \Rightarrow (x : \text{TypeG } i) \rightarrow Q \ i \ x$$

are all derived. We direct the reader to the formalization for the definition of these functions and the definition of the associated proof algebras [indind2/ind.ced]. Note that the proof algebras follow the same pattern as the efficient Mendler-style proof algebras of previous Cedille encodings [10]. Indeed, these inductive encodings *are* Mendler-style inductive types as they reduce, now through an additional layer, to Mendler-style indexed inductive data. An example of this encoding applied to CtxF and TyF where more standard induction principles are defined is also available [example.ced].

This second variant has the correct indices and has a smaller input burden. Of course, an elaborated definition would be able to impose a syntactic restriction to automatically derive monotonicity, but that is a price that must be paid for the additional flexibility of a semantic criterion of monotonicity.

4   Related and Future Work

Inductive-inductive definitions were studied extensively by Forsberg et al [12, 22]. Forsberg's thesis heavily inspired this work [11]. In particular, Forsberg describes an axiomatic description of inductive-inductive types and shows how to model them with indexed inductive types when using equality reflection (i.e. uniqueness of identity proofs and function extensionality). Moreover, his work is relative to a predicative theory and is presented via a theory of containers where inductive types are presented by a type of codes. Kaposi et al. expand on this reduction showing that inductive data are sufficient for finitary inductive-inductive types in Extensional Type Theory [17]. The first variant of the generic encoding we present differs from Forsberg's in that it does not use codes for types and instead impredicativity and does not require an equality reflection rule or function extensionality. Like Forsberg's translation (but not like his axiomatic description), our encoding is limited to "simple" inductive motives.

Quotient inductive-inductive types are an extension that have been demonstrated as a powerful technique for internalizing the definition of dependent type theories [2,5,16]. Our first generic variant is suggestively described as a *quotient*. Indeed, many constructions in Cedille via dependent intersection might fruitfully be cast in a framework of quotients. However, these kinds of quotients are through a normalization argument only and thus quotients such as multisets would not be possible. It is an open question if quotient inductive-inductive definitions could be generically encoded in Cedille using similar techniques. We conjecture that it is possible when the equivalence relation has decidable canonical elements.

Induction-recursion is another powerful technique for defining universes of type codes [6–8]. Cedille does not possess large eliminations natively because it does not possess inductive data natively. Thus, computing types by recursion is relegated to simulated computation rules or casts. However, these simulated large eliminations are encoded themselves via inductive definitions. It stands to reason that if a simulated large elimination is an inductive type already, that an inductive-inductive definition could yield a simulated inductive-recursive definition. Note that this is different from *small* induction-recursion where the recursive function computes a term instead of a type [14].

5   Conclusion

In this work we have shown how to encode inductive-inductive data in Cedille, a dependently typed programming language based on the Calculus of Constructions with three extensions. Our first generic encoding reduces inductive-inductive data to indexed inductive data by first defining the shape of the constructors and then a predicate to describe normal forms. Second, we demonstrate another framework that layers on the first and fixes redundancy and indices problems in the prior reduction. This is another installment in the story of encoding efficient inductive data in Cedille, and it is the authors' opinion that there is still a lot of potential left to be uncovered.

References

1. Allen, S.F., Bickford, M., Constable, R.L., Eaton, R., Kreitz, C., Lorigo, L., Moran, E.: Innovations in computational type theory using nuprl. J. Appl. Logic 4(4), 428–469 (2006)
2. Altenkirch, T., Capriotti, P., Dijkstra, G., Kraus, N., Nordvall Forsberg, F.: Quotient inductive-inductive types. In: Baier, C., Dal Lago, U. (eds.) FoSSaCS 2018. LNCS, vol. 10803, pp. 293–310. Springer, Cham (2018). https://doi.org/10.1007/978-3-319-89366-2_16

3. Altenkirch, T., Morris, P., Nordvall Forsberg, F., Setzer, A.: A categorical semantics for inductive-inductive definitions. In: Corradini, A., Klin, B., Cîrstea, C. (eds.) CALCO 2011. LNCS, vol. 6859, pp. 70–84. Springer, Heidelberg (2011). https://doi.org/10.1007/978-3-642-22944-2_6

4. Atkey, R.: Syntax and semantics of quantitative type theory. In: Proceedings of the 33rd Annual ACM/IEEE Symposium on Logic in Computer Science, pp. 56–65 (2018)

5. Dijkstra, G.: Quotient inductive-inductive definitions. Ph.D. thesis, University of Nottingham (2017)

6. Dybjer, P., Setzer, A.: A finite axiomatization of inductive-recursive definitions. In: Girard, J.-Y. (ed.) TLCA 1999. LNCS, vol. 1581, pp. 129–146. Springer, Heidelberg (1999). https://doi.org/10.1007/3-540-48959-2_11

7. Dybjer, P., Setzer, A.: Induction-recursion and initial algebras. Ann. Pure Appl. Logic **124**(1–3), 1–47 (2003)

8. Dybjer, P., Setzer, A.: Indexed induction-recursion. J. Logic Algebr. Program. **66**(1), 1–49 (2006)

9. Firsov, D., Blair, R., Stump, A.: Efficient Mendler-style lambda-encodings in cedille. In: Avigad, J., Mahboubi, A. (eds.) ITP 2018. LNCS, vol. 10895, pp. 235–252. Springer, Cham (2018). https://doi.org/10.1007/978-3-319-94821-8_14

10. Firsov, D., Blair, R., Stump, A.: Efficient mendler-style lambda-encodings in cedille. In: Interactive Theorem Proving: 9th International Conference, ITP 2018, Held as Part of the Federated Logic Conference, FloC 2018, Oxford, UK, 9–12 July 2018, Proceedings 9, pp. 235–252. Springer (2018)

11. Forsberg, F.N.: Inductive-inductive definitions. Ph.D. thesis, Swansea University (2013). http://login.proxy.lib.uiowa.edu/login?url=https://www.proquest.com/dissertations-theses/inductive-definitions/docview/2041902169/se-2 copyright - Database copyright ProQuest LLC; ProQuest does not claim copyright in the individual underlying works. Accessed 21 Oct 2022

12. Forsberg, F.N., Setzer, A.: A finite axiomatisation of inductive-inductive definitions. Logic Constr. Comput. **3**, 259–287 (2012)

13. Geuvers, H.: Induction is not derivable in second order dependent type theory. In: Abramsky, S. (ed.) TLCA 2001. LNCS, vol. 2044, pp. 166–181. Springer, Heidelberg (2001). https://doi.org/10.1007/3-540-45413-6_16

14. Hancock, P., McBride, C., Ghani, N., Malatesta, L., Altenkirch, T.: Small induction recursion. In: Hasegawa, M. (ed.) TLCA 2013. LNCS, vol. 7941, pp. 156–172. Springer, Heidelberg (2013). https://doi.org/10.1007/978-3-642-38946-7_13

15. Jenkins, C., Marmaduke, A., Stump, A.: Simulating large eliminations in cedille. In: Basold, H., Cockx, J., Ghilezan, S. (eds.) 27th International Conference on Types for Proofs and Programs (TYPES 2021). Leibniz International Proceedings in Informatics (LIPIcs), vol. 239, pp. 9:1–9:22. Schloss Dagstuhl - Leibniz-Zentrum für Informatik, Dagstuhl, Germany (2022). https://doi.org/10.4230/LIPIcs.TYPES.2021.9, https://drops.dagstuhl.de/opus/volltexte/2022/16778

16. Kaposi, A., Kovács, A., Altenkirch, T.: Constructing quotient inductive-inductive types. Proc. ACM Program. Lang. **3**(POPL), 1–24 (2019)

17. Kaposi, A., Kovács, A., Lafont, A.: For finitary induction-induction, induction is enough. In: TYPES 2019: 25th International Conference on Types for Proofs and Programs, vol. 175, pp. 6–1. Schloss Dagstuhl-Leibniz-Zentrum für Informatik (2019)

18. Kaposi, A., von Raumer, J.: A syntax for mutual inductive families (2020)

19. Kopylov, A.: Dependent intersection: a new way of defining records in type theory. In: Proceedings of the 18th Annual IEEE Symposium on Logic in Computer Science, LICS 2003, pp. 86–95.IEEE Computer Society, Washington, DC (2003)
20. Marmaduke, A., Jenkins, C., Stump, A.: Quotients by idempotent functions in cedille. In: Bowman, W.J., Garcia, R. (eds.) TFP 2019. LNCS, vol. 12053, pp. 1–20. Springer, Cham (2020). https://doi.org/10.1007/978-3-030-47147-7_1
21. Miquel, A.: The implicit calculus of constructions extending pure type systems with an intersection type binder and subtyping. In: Abramsky, S. (ed.) TLCA 2001. LNCS, vol. 2044, pp. 344–359. Springer, Heidelberg (2001). https://doi.org/10.1007/3-540-45413-6_27
22. Nordvall Forsberg, F., Setzer, A.: Inductive-inductive definitions. In: Dawar, A., Veith, H. (eds.) CSL 2010. LNCS, vol. 6247, pp. 454–468. Springer, Heidelberg (2010). https://doi.org/10.1007/978-3-642-15205-4_35
23. Parigot, M.: Programming with proofs: a second order type theory. In: Ganzinger, H. (ed.) ESOP 1988. LNCS, vol. 300, pp. 145–159. Springer, Heidelberg (1988). https://doi.org/10.1007/3-540-19027-9_10
24. Parigot, M.: On the representation of data in lambda-calculus. In: Börger, E., Büning, H.K., Richter, M.M. (eds.) CSL 1989. LNCS, vol. 440, pp. 309–321. Springer, Heidelberg (1990). https://doi.org/10.1007/3-540-52753-2_47
25. Stump, A.: The calculus of dependent lambda eliminations. J. Funct. Program. **27**, e14 (2017)
26. Stump, A.: From realizability to induction via dependent intersection. Ann. Pure Appl. Logic **169**(7), 637–655 (2018). https://doi.org/10.1016/j.apal.2018.03.002

Versatile and Flexible Modelling of the RISC-V Instruction Set Architecture

Sören Tempel[1]([⊠]) [iD], Tobias Brandt[2] [iD], and Christoph Lüth[1,3] [iD]

[1] University of Bremen, 28359 Bremen, Germany
tempel@uni-bremen.de
[2] Bremen, Germany
[3] Deutsches Forschungszentrum für Künstliche Intelligenz (DFKI),
28359 Bremen, Germany
christoph.lueth@dfki.de

Abstract. Formal languages are commonly used to model the semantics of instruction set architectures (*e.g.* ARM). The majority of prior work on these formal languages focuses on concrete instruction execution and validation tasks. We present a novel Haskell-based modelling approach which allows the creation of flexible and versatile architecture models based on free monads and a custom expression language. Contrary to existing work, our approach does not make any assumptions regarding the representation of memory and register values. This way, we can implement non-concrete software analysis techniques (*e.g.* symbolic execution where values are SMT expressions) on top of our model as interpreters for this model. In contrast to prior work, our modelling approach is therefore explicitly focused on the creation of custom ISA interpreters. We employ our outlined approach to create an abstract model and a concrete interpreter for the RISC-V base instruction set. Based on this model, we demonstrate that custom interpreters can be implemented with minimal effort using dynamic information flow tracking as a case study.

1 Introduction and Motivation

An instruction set architecture (ISA) describes the instructions of a processor, its state (number and types of registers), its memory, and more. It is the central interface between hard- and software, and as such of crucial importance; once fixed, it cannot be easily changed anymore. Traditionally, ISAs were specified in natural language, but that has been found lacking in exactness and completeness. Therefore, modelling an ISA, in particular a novel one, with formal languages has become *de rigeur*. Functional languages can be put to good use here: because of their declarative nature, we can formulate the behaviour at an abstract level which at the same time is executable.

Research supported by the German Federal Ministry of Education and Research (BMBF) under grant no. 01IW22002 (ECXL) and grant no. 16ME0127 (Scale4Edge).

S. Chang (Ed.): TFP 2023, LNCS 13868, pp. 16–35, 2023.
https://doi.org/10.1007/978-3-031-38938-2_2

Recently, the RISC-V ISA [15, 16] has emerged has an attractive alternative to the prevailing industry standards, such as the Intel x86 or ARM architecture. It is open source, patent-free, and designed to be scalable from embedded devices to servers. Its open nature has sparked a lot of research activity, in particular many formal models of the ISA, including some in Haskell [3, 12, 17], or in custom domain-specific languages (DSLs) such as SAIL [1]. An *executable model* of the ISA is a simulator, *i.e.* software which simulates the behaviour of programs as faithful to the hardware as possible. As such, an ISA simulator is essentially an *interpreter* for machine code (*i.e.* software in binary form).

Our contribution as presented here is a highly flexible and versatile model of the RISC-V ISA in Haskell. As opposed to existing models, the interpretation of the ISA can be varied. To this end, we define an embedded domain-specific language (EDSL) via a free monad construction. The idea is that the free monad models the computation given by a sequence of operations from the ISA, where the model of computation (*i.e.* the interpretation) can be varied, from simple state transitions which simulate the ISA faithfully, to sophisticated analyses such as symbolic execution [2] or dynamic information flow tracking [21]. While prior work on formal ISA models focuses largely on validation tasks, our model is specifically centered around the implementation of custom interpreters. To the best of our knowledge, our approach is therefore the first which enables the creation of software analysis tools (e.g. symbolic execution) as interpreters for the formal ISA model. By building these tools on top of an abstract model, we can (1) easily extend the analysis to additional instructions,[1] (2) analyse software written in any programming language that compiles to machine-code for the modelled ISA, and (3) potentially ease proofing the correctness of these analyses tools by leveraging existing proof-assistant definitions for ISA semantics. Our work is motivated by our experience with `riscv-vp` [7], an existing RISC-V simulator written in C++ using SystemC TLM [23]. After having to modify `riscv-vp` repeatedly to allow such analyses [13, 25, 26], we were looking for a more systematic and structured way to achieve this flexibility. The case study we have conducted with an exemplary implementation of dynamic information flow tracking for RISC-V machine code illustrates the feasibility of our approach for this purpose. Furthermore, performed experiments indicate that interpreters based on our formal model are able to compete with `riscv-vp` in terms of simulation speed.

The remainder of article is structured as follows: we first provide background information on instruction set architectures and the free monad abstraction. We then demonstrate how to model a very simple ISA to motivate our model of the real RISC-V ISA which we present in Sect. 4 and leverage to implement a custom interpreter as a case study. In Sect. 5 we evaluate the performance (*i.e.* simulation speed) of our implementation, and in Sect. 6 we compare our approach to related work. Lastly, we discuss opportunities for future work and provide a conclusion.

---

[1] This is paramount for modular ISAs (like RISC-V) where different instruction set extensions can be combined, thereby, requiring the analysis tool to support them.

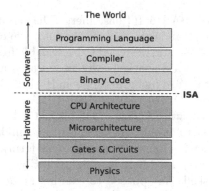

Fig. 1. Relation of the ISA to other software and hardware abstraction layers.

2 Preliminaries

In the following, we provide background information on instruction set architectures and the free monad abstraction as a prerequisite for the following sections.

2.1 Instruction Set Architectures

As illustrated in Fig. 1, the ISA is the central interface between the hard- and software and conceptually forms the boundary between the two. In order to allow the software to interact with the hardware, the ISA specifies the instruction encoding for binary code and the semantics of said instructions. Software in high-level programming languages (such as C++ or Haskell) is translated by a compiler to binary code which then uses the instructions of a specific ISA (*e.g.* x86, ARM, or RISC-V). These instructions are then implemented in hardware by the CPU. As software is commonly loaded into memory, the CPU must fetch the next instruction from memory and decode it before executing it. This process is commonly referred to as the *fetch-decode-execute cycle* [20, Sect. 14.3].

Different instruction set architectures exist. In this paper we are generally focusing on load-store architectures where operands to instructions are registers. That is, operations on memory values can only be performed by first loading them into registers, performing an operation on them, and then storing them in memory again [20, Sect. 14.6]. Load-store data processing is widely used by so-called reduced instruction set computer (RISC) architectures (*e.g.* RISC-V) which are focused on simplicity of standardized instructions [20, Sect. 15.4].

An ISA is in essence a low-level imperative programming language with pre-defined bit-vector data types (words of given length). In order to execute or analyse software in binary form (*e.g.* in a simulator or a dynamic binary software analysis tool), one needs to implement an interpreter for the ISA. Ideally, such an implementation should be flexible in the sense that it can be re-used for different execution and analysis tasks without having to re-implement the entirety of the ISA each time. Prior work on imperative programs has leveraged monadic abstractions for this purpose; more about this in the following section.

2.2 Free Monads

The semantics of imperative programs has many aspects (stateful computations, continuations, exception) each of which can be modelled in Haskell using monads; combining these monads is a notoriously tricky exercise. Early work on interpreting imperative programs used monad transformers for this effect [11], but more recent work uses free monads for better performance and extensibility (see Subsect. 6.2 for a detailed comparison); we sketch the basic concepts here.

A free monad for a type constructor f is essentially the closure of f under application (it contains arbitrarily many applications of f); the appeal is that we can define the monad separately for each constructor of f, allowing to write EDSLs in a modular way. The category-theoretic construction of free monads was given by Kelly [8], and first described in the context of functional programming by Swierstra [22]. In its simplest form, the free monad is given as:

```
data Free f a = Pure a | Free (f (Free f a))
```

In our implementation, we use an enhanced version of this concept. Further details on the exact implementation are provided in the appendix (Sect. A).

3   Modelling an ISA

We motivate our approach and its advantages by applying it to a very simple ISA. The ISA implements a 32-bit load-store architecture with five instructions; each of these can be thought of as representing a class of similar instructions in a real ISA:

1. LOADI *imm reg*: Load immediate into register *reg*.
2. ADD *dst src1 src2*: Add two registers into *dst*.
3. LW *dest addr*: Load word from memory at *addr* into register *dest*.
4. SW *addr src*: Store word from register *src* into memory at *addr*.
5. BEQ *reg1 reg2 off*: Relative branch by *off* if registers *reg1* and *reg2* are equal.

The ISA supports 16 general-purpose registers, word-addressable memory, and a program counter which points to the current instruction in memory. All registers and memory values are 32-bit wide and treated as signed values by all instructions. Instruction fetching and decoding is not discussed. The instruction set is modelled straightforward as a Haskell data type (where Word and Addr are type synonyms for 32-bit integers):

```
newtype Reg = Reg { reg :: Int } deriving (Ord, Eq)
data INSTR
    = LOADI Word Reg
    | ADD Reg Reg Reg
    | LW Reg Addr
    | SW Addr Reg
    | BEQ Reg Reg Word
```

```
type System = (Registers              type System' = (Registers
            , Mem                                  , Mem
            , ProgramCounter)                      , ProgramCounter
                                                   , Int)

execute :: INSTR → State System ()    execute' :: INSTR → State System' ()
execute i = modify $                  execute' i = modify $
 λ(regs, mem, pc) → case i of          λ(regs, mem, pc, counter) → case i of
  LOADI imm r → (insert r imm regs,     LOADI imm r → (insert r imm regs, mem,
                mem, nextInstr pc)                    nextInstr pc, counter)
  ADD rd rs1 rs2 → let                  ADD rd rs1 rs2 → let
     v1 = regs ! rs1                       v1 = regs ! rs1
     v2 = regs ! rs2                       v2 = regs ! rs2
    in  (insert rd (v1+v2) regs,         in (insert rd (v1+v2) regs,
         mem, nextInstr pc)                  mem, nextInstr pc, counter)
  LW r addr → let                       LW r addr → let
     w = mem ! addr                        w = mem ! addr
    in  (insert r w regs, mem,           in (insert r w regs, mem,
         nextInstr pc)                       nextInstr pc, succ counter)
  SW addr r → let                       SW addr r → let
     v = regs ! r                          v = regs ! r
    in (regs, insert addr v mem,         in (regs, insert addr v mem,
        nextInstr pc)                        nextInstr pc, succ counter)
  BEQ r1 r2 off → let                   BEQ r1 r2 off → let
     v1 = regs ! r1                        v1 = regs ! r1
     v2 = regs ! r2                        v2 = regs ! r2
     br = if v1 == v2                      br = if v1 == v2
        then pc+off                          then pc+off
        else nextInstr pc                    else nextInstr pc
    in (regs, mem, br)                   in (regs, mem, br, counter)
```

Listing 1.1. Concrete Haskell model   **Listing 1.2.** Memory accesses analysis

3.1 A First Model

The execution model formally describes how instructions are executed. It specifies the system state, and how instructions change the system state (including the control flow).

Listing 1.1 provides a simple Haskell execution model for our exemplary ISA. The architectural state System, upon which instructions are executed, is a tuple consisting of two finite maps for the memory and register file as well as a concrete program counter. Instruction execution itself is implemented as a pure function which performs a pattern match on the instruction type and returns a new system state, embedded into a state monad (State System α).

Unfortunately, this simple ISA model has several shortcomings. Consider a simple software analysis task for which we want to extend our model to track the number of memory accesses during program execution. For this, we merely need to extend the system state with an access counter, and increment the counter whenever memory access takes place (operations LW and SW). A possible implementation of this modification is shown in Listing 1.2. Note how, even though our extension to the previous solution did not modify the control flow of the program in any way, we still had to restate the control flow for all supported instructions of our ISA. For our small ISA this inconvenience seem feasible, but considering that a real ISA has often more than 80 instructions, the task of modifying the execution becomes cumbersome and error-prone.

Hence, our aim is to give a modular, abstract representation of ISA semantics, based upon which we can then implement software analysis techniques which require a different kind of interpretation with minimal effort. Such techniques may include symbolic execution [2] or dynamic information flow tracking [21].

3.2 Our Approach

The problem with the previously outlined approach is that the model of the semantics (a state transition given by a state monad) is given in a very concrete and monolithic form: there is no separation between the different aspects of the semantics. However, the semantics of an ISA has several aspects: memory access, register access, arithmetic, and control flow, and most analyses only concern one or two of them (*e.g.* memory access, or arithmetic). Yet, if we want to change the representation of the state, this affects all operations; similarly if we want to reason about *e.g.* integer arithmetic to show absence of integer overflow, we need to re-implement all operations.

Thus, we want to give the semantics of our ISA by combining several consti-tuting parts, which we can change individually. To this end, we define an EDSL which represents the operations of an abstract machine implementing the ISA, *e.g.* loading and storing words into registers, using a free monad as introduced in Subsect. 2.2.

```
data Operations r
  = LoadRegister Reg (Word → r)
  | StoreRegister Reg Word r
  | IncrementPC Word r
  | LoadMem Addr (Word → r)
  | StoreMem Addr Word r
  deriving Functor

loadRegister :: Reg → Free Operations Word
loadRegister r = Free (LoadRegister r Pure)

storeRegister :: Reg → Word → Free Operations ()
storeRegister r w = Free (StoreRegister r w (Pure ()))

incrementPC :: Word → Free Operations ()
incrementPC v = Free (IncrementPC v (Pure ()))

loadMem :: Addr → Free Operations Word
loadMem addr = Free (LoadMem addr Pure)

storeMem :: Addr → Word → Free Operations ()
storeMem addr w = Free (StoreMem addr w (Pure ()))
```
Listing 1.3. EDSL of the machine executing the ISA

The operations comprising the EDSL are given by a parameterized data type `Operations`, see Listing 1.3[2]. The `Operations` data type models the ISA in abstract terms; the free monad `Free Operations` describes combinations of these, which are an abstract representation of the control flow of a (sequence of) ISA operations. This representation is given by a function `controlFlow :: INSTR →` `Free Operations ()`, which defines the control flow for a given instruction (see Listing 1.4); by composing these we get the control flow for a program (sequence of operations).

```
controlFlow :: INSTR → Free Operations ()
controlFlow = λcase
    LOADI imm r → storeRegister r imm ≫ incrementPC instrSize
    ADD rd r1 r2 → do
        v1 ← loadRegister r1
        v2 ← loadRegister r2
        storeRegister rd (v1+v2)
        incrementPC instrSize
    LW r addr → do
        v ← loadMem addr
        storeRegister r v
        incrementPC instrSize
    SW addr r → do
        v ← loadRegister r
        storeMem addr v
        incrementPC instrSize
    BEQ r1 r2 off → do
        v1 ← loadRegister r1
        v2 ← loadRegister r2
        if v1 ≡ v2 then incrementPC off else incrementPC instrSize
```

Listing 1.4. Interpreting an in ISA instruction in the free monad.

To reconstruct the concrete execution of the ISA instructions from the previous section (Listing 1.1), we need to map the operations in the free monad to concrete monadic effects, in our case in Haskell's pure `State` monad. An example implementation of a function which performs this mapping is provided in Listing 1.5.

```
execute :: State → Free Operations () → State
execute st = flip execState st ∘ iterM go where
    go = λcase
        LoadRegister reg f → gets (λ(rs,_,_) → rs ! reg) ≫= f
        StoreRegister reg w c →
            modify (λ(rs, mem, pc) → (insert reg w rs, mem, pc)) ≫ c
        IncrementPC w c → modify (λ(rs,mem,pc) → (rs,mem,pc+w)) ≫ c
        LoadMem addr f  → gets (λ(_,mem,_) → mem ! addr) ≫= f
        StoreMem addr w c →
            modify (λ(rs,mem,pc) → (rs, insert addr w mem, pc)) ≫ c
```

Listing 1.5. Evaluating the control flow using the `State` monad

---

[2] For convenience, we add a smart-constructor for each constructor of the data type.

Since we have now separated control flow and semantics of effects, we could also use any other (monadic) effects for the evaluation without changing the control flow. Reconstructing the example from Listing 1.2 just requires adjustments in the semantics without restating the control flow as shown in Listing 1.6 (performed adjustments are highlighted using red text color).

```
execute' :: State" → Free Operations () → State"
execute' st = flip execState st ∘ iterM go where
    go = λcase
        LoadRegister reg f → gets (λ(rs,_,_,_) → rs ! reg) ≫=f
        StoreRegister reg w c → modify
            (λ(rs, mem, pc, counter) →
                (insert reg w rs, mem, pc, counter)) ≫ c
        IncrementPC w c → modify
            (λ(rs, mem, pc, counter) → (rs,mem,pc+w,counter)) ≫ c
        LoadMem addr f  → do
            v ← gets (λ(_,mem,_, counter) → mem ! addr)
            modify (λ(rs,mem,pc,counter) → (rs, mem, pc, succ counter))
            f v
        StoreMem addr w c →
            modify (λ(rs,mem,pc,counter) →
                (rs, insert addr w mem, pc, succ counter)) ≫ c
```

Listing 1.6. Executing and counting memory accesses

While this is a major advantage in terms of reusability, there is still room for improvement. In particular, we are not able to change the semantics of the expression-level calculations an operation performs, since the data type of our EDSL assumes concrete types, which entails they are already evaluated. Hence, we generalize our Operations to allow a representation of the evaluation of expressions, much like we did for the instructions (except that the evaluation of expressions is not monadic, hence we do not need a free monad here). For that, we need to introduce a simple expression language, which will replace all the constant values, e.g. the constructor StoreRegister :: Reg → Word → r becomes StoreRegister' :: Reg → Expr w → r, as well as adjust the Operations type such that it becomes polymorphic in the word type.

Listing 1.7 shows the changes necessary, e.g. the execute''' function is now provided with an expression-interpreter evalE, which is used to evaluate expressions generated by the control flow. The Operations are now polymorphic in the word-type and the semantics of the internal computations can be changed by adjusting evalE; this allows our approach to be used to implement various software analysis techniques on the ISA level. In the next section, we will present an application of our approach to the RISC-V ISA, and utilize the resulting RISC-V model to implement one exemplary software analysis technique as a case study.

```
data Expr a = Val a | Add (Expr a) (Expr a) | Eq (Expr a) (Expr a)

data Operations' w r
    = LoadRegister' Reg (Expr w → r)
    | StoreRegister' Reg (Expr w) r
```

```
    | IncrementPC' (Expr w) r
    | LoadMem' Addr (Expr w → r)
    | StoreMem' Addr (Expr w) r

evalE :: Expr Word → Word
evalE = λcase
    Val a → a
    Add e e' → evalE e + evalE e'
    Eq e e' → if evalE e' == evalE e then 1 else 0

execute''' :: (Expr Word → Word) → State''
                → Free (Operations' Word) () → State''
execute''' evalE st = flip execState st ∘ iterM go where
    go = λcase
        LoadRegister' reg f → gets (λ(rs,_,_,_) → Val $ rs ! reg) >>= f
        StoreRegister' reg w c → modify
            (λ(rs, mem, pc, counter) →
                (insert reg (evalE w) rs, mem, pc, counter)) >> c
        IncrementPC' w c → modify
            (λ(rs,mem,pc,counter) → (rs,mem,pc+ evalE w, counter)) >> c
        LoadMem' addr f → do
            v ← gets (λ(_,mem,_, counter) → mem ! addr)
            modify (λ(rs,mem,pc,counter) → (rs, mem, pc, succ counter))
            f $ Val v
        StoreMem' addr w c → modify (λ(rs,mem,pc,counter)
            → (rs, insert addr (evalE w) mem, pc, succ counter)) >> c
```

Listing 1.7. Operations type with simple expression language

4   Modelling the RISC-V ISA

As an application of our approach, we created an abstract model of the RISC-V ISA. RISC-V is an emerging RISC architecture which has recently gained traction in both academia and industry. Contrary to existing ISAs, RISC-V is developed as an open standard free from patents and royalties. It is designed in a modular way: the architecture consists of a base instructions set and optional extensions (*e.g.* for atomic instructions) which can be combined as needed [15].

We refer to our model of the RISC-V architecture as LIBRISCV. As the name suggests, LIBRISCV is a Haskell library which can be used to implement different interpreters for RISC-V software. As such, the library provides an instantiable framework for versatile interpretation of RISC-V software in binary form. Figure 2 illustrates how the concepts from Subsect. 3.2 are applied to RISC-V in order to achieve versatile interpretation. The figure will be further described in the following subsections.

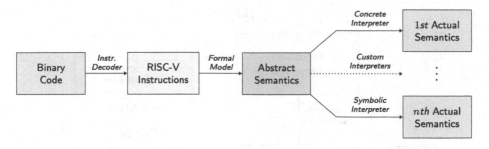

Fig. 2. Application of our ISA modelling approach to the RISC-V architecture.

4.1 Instruction Decoder

As depicted in Fig. 2, our RISC-V implementation receives binary code as an input value. This binary code constitutes RISC-V machine code and is converted to an algebraic data structure representing instructions mandated by the RISC-V standard using an instruction decoder. Contrary to imperative programming languages, execution and decoding/parsing is heavily intertwined for machine code. As discussed in Subsect. 2.1, we can only decode the next instruction after finishing execution of the current instruction. For example, when executing a branch instruction the next fetched instruction depends on the result of the branch. We make use of lazy evaluation to model the fetch-decode-execute cycle as part of our control flow description. That is, the fetching of the next instruction is itself—non-strictly—modelled, using free monads as outlined in Subsect. 3.2.

Contrary to existing work, a description of RISC-V instruction decoding is not part of our EDSL. Instead, the LIBRISCV instruction decoder is automatically generated from `riscv-opcodes`[3], an existing formal language which describes how binary code is mapped to RISC-V instructions (without modelling instruction semantics). Based on algebraic data types, returned by the instruction decoder, we specify the *abstract semantics* of RISC-V instructions through a formal ISA model described in the following.

4.2 Formal Model

An overview of the ISA model provided by LIBRISCV is available in Fig. 3. As illustrated in Fig. 2, the central component of the formal model is the description of the abstract instruction semantics which represents the lazily-generated control flow of the RISC-V ISA operations. As discussed in Subsect. 3.2, we use free monads for this purpose. For the implementation of free monads, we use the `freer-simple` library[4]. The library provides an improved implementation of the free monad approach described in the appendix (Sect. A). Within the

---

[3] https://github.com/riscv/riscv-opcodes.
[4] https://hackage.haskell.org/package/freer-simple.

LIBRISCV

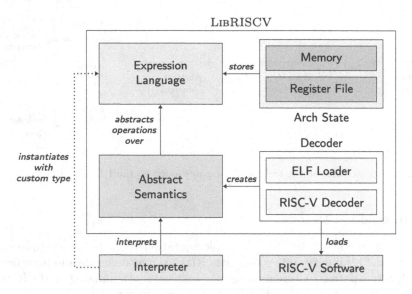

Fig. 3. Overview of the RISC-V ISA model provided by LIBRISCV.

abstract description of instruction semantics, all operations on register/memory values are abstracted using a generic expression language. The expression language is implemented as an algebraic data type with an associated evaluation function, as illustrated in Listing 1.7. The algebraic data type, used by the expression language, is parameterized over a custom type. The architectural state (*i.e.* memory and register file) is also parameterized over this type. As shown in Fig. 3, the abstract description of instruction semantics is based on an instruction type which is generated by the aforementioned instruction decoder. The decoder is responsible for loading RISC-V software in the Executable and Linkable Format (ELF) and for decoding/parsing instruction words—contained in the file—according to the RISC-V specification.

Based on the abstract semantics, we can provide different interpreters which implement the *actual semantics* for decoded RISC-V instructions as illustrated in Fig. 2, such as concrete or symbolic execution of modelled instructions. The actual semantics implement the state transition for each modelled instruction while the abstract semantics only describe the control flow. Each interpreter instantiates the expression language with a type. Based on this type, an interpreter for the formal ISA model (*i.e.* the expression language and the free Operations monad) needs to be supplied. Presently, LIBRISCV provides a formal model for the 32-bit variant of the RISC-V base instruction set (40 instructions). Based on this formal model, we have implemented a concrete interpreter for RISC-V instructions. Both the model and the concrete interpreter are written in roughly 1500 LOC and can be obtained from GitHub[5]. Using the concrete interpreter, we were able to successfully execute and pass the official RISC-V

---

[5] https://github.com/agra-uni-bremen/libriscv.

ISA tests for the 32-bit base instruction set[6]. These tests include multiple test programs (one for each instruction) which check if the implemented behavior of an instruction conforms to the specification. Passing these tests indicates that our model correctly captures the semantics of the base instruction set. In the following, we illustrate how custom interpreters—beyond the standard concrete interpretation—can be implemented on top of our abstract model, thereby making use of its flexibility.

4.3   Custom Interpreters

Our model of the RISC-V ISA is designed for maximum flexibility and versatility, along the lines sketched in Subsect. 3.2. This allows implementing different interpretations of the ISA on top of our abstract model with minimal effort. Conceptually, each custom interpreter implements actual semantics for the abstract semantics provided by the formal ISA model (see Fig. 2). In order to implement a custom RISC-V interpreter, an evaluator for the expression language and an interpreter for the free Operations monad need to be provided. As an example, dynamic information flow tracking [21], where data-flow from input to output is analysed, can be implemented using the following polymorphic data type:

```
data Tainted a = MkTainted Bool a

instance Conversion (Tainted a) a where
    convert (MkTainted _ v) = v
```

The product type Tainted tracks whether a value of type a is subject to data-flow analysis. Furthermore, a conversion to Word32 is implemented through an instance-declaration for the Tainted type. This conversion is the only class constraint imposed by our abstract model on the type used by the custom interpreter.[7] An evaluator of the expression language for Tainted Word32 can be implemented as follows:[8]

```
evalE :: Expr (Tainted Word32) → Tainted Word32
evalE (FromImm t) = t
evalE (FromInt i) = MkTainted False $ fromIntegral i
evalE (AddU e1 e2) = MkTainted (t1 || t2) $ v1 + v2
    where (MkTainted t1 v1) = evalE e1; (MkTainted t2 v2) = evalE e2
```

The evaluator performs standard concrete integer arithmetic on the Word32 encapsulated within the Tainted type. However, if one of the operands of the arithmetic operations is a tainted value, then the resulting value is also tainted. This enables a simple data-flow analysis for initially tainted values. Based on the evaluation function, an interpretation of the control flow is shown in the following, where $f \rightsquigarrow g$ denotes a natural transformation from f to g (as provided by the freer-simple library):

---

[6] https://github.com/riscv/riscv-tests.

[7] This constraint is necessary as the instruction decoder operates on Word32 values.

[8] The FromImm, FromInt, and AddU constructors belong to our expression abstraction.

```
type ArchState = ( REG.RegisterFile IOArray (Tainted Word32)
                 , MEM.Memory IOArray (Tainted Word8))

type IftEnv = (Expr (Tainted Word32) → Tainted Word32, ArchState)

iftBehaviour :: IftEnv → Free Operations (Tainted Word32) ⤳ IO
iftBehaviour (evalE , (regFile, mem)) = λcase
    (ReadRegister idx) → REG.readRegister regFile idx
    (WriteRegister idx reg) → REG.writeRegister regFile idx (evalE reg)
    (LoadWord addr) → MEM.loadWord mem (convert $ evalE addr)
    (StoreWord addr w) → MEM.storeWord mem (convert $ evalE addr)
                                          (evalE w)
```

This function operates on a polymorphic register and memory implementation. Expressions are evaluated using evalE, and then written to the register file or memory. When execution terminates, we can inspect each register and memory value to check whether it depends on an initially tainted input value. As shown, the interpreter only implements a subset of the Operations monad and the expression language; a complete implementation is provided in the example/ subdirectory on GitHub. We have already implemented dynamic information flow tracking for RISC-V machine code in prior work based on the riscv-vp simulator mentioned in Sect. 1 [13]. For this prior implementation, we had to modify riscv-vp extensively to allow for such an analysis to be performed, as it does not separate instruction semantics from instruction execution. In this context, the case study provided here serves to demonstrate that such techniques can be more easily implemented on top of an abstract formal model as custom interpreters for this model.

5   Performance Evaluation

Free monads introduce a well-known performance problem [9, Sect. 2.6] (see Sect. A). As our approach is focused on implementing interpreters, simulation performance is important when executing real-world software. To evaluate simulation speed, we conduct a comparison with existing RISC-V simulators and specifically quantify the impact of the utilized freer-simple library on simulation performance. For this purpose, we leverage the existing Embench 1.0 benchmark suite [6]. Embench contains several benchmark applications which perform different computation-intensive tasks (e.g. checksum calculation). We compiled all applications for the 32-bit RISC-V base instruction set, executed them with different RISC-V simulators, and measured execution time in seconds. The results are shown in Table 1. All experiments have been conducted on an Intel Xeon Gold 6240 running an Alpine Linux 3.17 Docker image. Artefacts for the performed evaluation are available on Zenodo [24].

For each benchmark application in Table 1, we list the execution time in seconds for different RISC-V simulators. In order to specifically quantify the performance impact of the freer-simple library, we use a modified version of LIBRISCV as a

Table 1. Execution time comparison in seconds with existing RISC-V simulators.

Benchmark	baseline	libriscv	forvis	grift	riscv-vp
aha-mont64	21.68	41.32	53.81	351.85	14.15
crc32	8.71	16.61	21.08	148.69	5.75
cubic	28.8	57.99	71.9	614.11	19.2
edn	80.16	160.36	193.93	1680.24	53.62
huffbench	8.31	15.41	20.18	108.62	5.6
matmult-int	41.71	82.72	96.94	820.24	28.07
minver	13.87	26.93	33.87	272.13	9.16
nbody	24.55	48.85	58.78	529.97	16.5
nettle-aes	8.91	16.19	19.99	118.77	5.93
nettle-sha256	6.94	12.5	15.68	89.82	4.43
nsichneu	4.19	7.63	9.3	59.18	2.79
picojpeg	13.99	26.3	38.66	203.55	9.73
qrduino	11.85	23.33	30.91	200.08	8.52
sglib-combined	7.94	14.33	18.52	106.38	5.24
slre	6.82	12.56	15.88	91.89	4.55
st	16.18	32.48	38.65	344.91	10.94
statemate	1.69	3.26	5.2	23.68	1.39
ud	14.44	27.1	33.47	222.35	9.42
wikisort	7.57	14.49	18.32	136.27	5.09
Geometric mean	12.072	23.02	29.372	197.959	8.161

baseline where we manually removed the dependency on `freer-simple` and evaluate the ISA directly in Haskell's IO-monad. As such, this baseline version is conceptually similar to the primitive model presented in Subsect. 3.1, *i.e.* the interpretation cannot be varied and it unconditionally performs concrete execution of RISC-V instructions. To contextualize the obtained results, we performed further experiments with existing Haskell implementations of the RISC-V ISA, namely Forvis [3] and GRIFT [17]. Contrary to our own work, these implementations do not utilize free monads (see Sect. 6). Lastly, Table 1 also contains evaluation results for the aforementioned `riscv-vp`, which is written in the C++ programming language [7]. To summarize benchmark results, Table 1 provides the geometric mean on a per-simulator basis in the bottom row.

Naturally, the C++ implementation (`riscv-vp`) has the lowest execution time over all benchmark applications. On average, it is roughly three times faster than our own Haskell implementation of the RISC-V ISA (LiBRISCV). This is to be expected as, contrary to Haskell, C++ is not garbage collected. Nonetheless, and despite the employment of free monads, LiBRISCV is—on average—still faster than Forvis and GRIFT. While LiBRISCV and Forvis have similar execution time results, GRIFT is significantly slower even though it is also written in Haskell. We attribute this to the fact that GRIFT employs a bit-vector expression language, as an additional abstraction layer, to perform operations on register/ memory values. The performance impact of the free monad abstraction (used in

LIBRISCV) can be estimated by comparing simulation performance with the baseline column in Table 1. As discussed above, the baseline column represents execution time for a LIBRISCV variant which does not use the `freer-simple` library. The gathered data indicates that LIBRISCV is two times slower than the baseline version, confirming that free monads have a significant impact on simulation performance. Nonetheless, LIBRISCV is still faster than existing Haskell implementations (Forvis and GRIFT) and approximately only three times slower than a primitive C++ implementation (`riscv-vp`). As such, we believe the induced performance penalty to be acceptable for our use case as the advantages of free monads outweigh this disadvantage by far.

6 Related Work

In the following, we discuss related work on formal ISA semantics, modular interpreters for imperative programming languages, and software analysis tools.

6.1 Formal Specifications

Formal semantics for ISAs is an active research area with a vast body of existing research. Specifically regarding RISC-V, a public review of existing formal specifications has been conducted by the RISC-V foundation in 2019 [14]. From this review, SAIL [1] emerged as the official formal specification for the RISC-V architecture. SAIL is a custom DSL for describing different ISAs and comes with tooling for automatically generating simulators from this description. However, we believe a functional specification in a programming language like Haskell to be more suitable for rapid prototyping of custom interpreters. Similar to our own work, existing work on GRIFT [17], Forvis [3], and riscv-semantics [12] models the RISC-V ISA using a Haskell EDSL. Forvis and riscv-semantics are explicitly designed for readability and thus only use a subset of Haskell. As opposed to our own work, instructions are executed directly and this prior work does not separate the description of instruction semantics from their execution. In this regard, GRIFT is closer to our own work as it uses a bit-vector expression language to provide a separate description of instruction semantics. However, GRIFT's expression language is designed around natural numbers as it focuses on concrete execution. For this reason, it is not possible to represent register/memory values abstractly using GRIFT (*i.e.* not as natural numbers, but for example as SMT expressions). To the best of our knowledge, our formal RISC-V model is the first executable model which focuses specifically on flexibility and thereby enables non-concrete execution of RISC-V instructions.

6.2 Modular Interpreters

Early work on modular interpreters for imperative languages [11] used *monad transformers* to compose the monads used to interpret the imperative features in a modular way. Monad transformers can be thought of as monads with a hole;

instead of a monad m modelling a feature f (say, stateful computation), we give a monad transformer m' modelling the addition of feature f to an existing monad. This allows us to combine features in a "stack" of monads, and is implemented in Haskell in the mtl library[9].

However, this approach has three drawbacks: firstly, the monad transformer already specifies the interaction with the other monad, so the approach is not truly compositional; secondly, it is not truly extensible, as once the monad stack is composed, no more monads can be added (this would result in a new monad stack); and thirdly, there is a severe performance cost for larger monad stacks [9, Sect. 4]. For these reasons, we use free monads with extensible effects which do not suffer from these drawbacks as explained in Sect. A, even though lowering the performance penalty of free monads (*cf.* Sect. 5) is still an open challenge.

Our work is intended as a framework for abstract interpretation on machine code. Leveraging monads for this purpose, it is related to work on monadic abstract interpreters [18]. Besides the use of monad transformers in that work, there is one crucial difference: for software, abstract interpretation techniques extract the control flow graph (CFG) of the program ([18] uses continuation-passing style semantics for this). We model the control flow implicitly using lazy evaluation; the next instruction is only fetched and decoded once it is needed.

6.3 Binary Software Analysis

Due to the utilization of free monads, we believe our RISC-V ISA model to be a versatile tool for implementing dynamic software analysis techniques that operate directly on the machine code level. Prior work has already demonstrated that it is feasible to implement techniques such as symbolic execution [26] or dynamic information flow tracking [13] for RISC-V machine code. However, this prior work does not leverage functional ISA specifications and thus relies on manual modifications of existing interpreters and is not easily applicable to additional RISC-V extensions or other ISAs (ARM, MIPS, . . .). For this reason, the majority of existing work on binary software analysis does not operate directly on the machine code level and instead leverages intermediate languages and lifts machine code to these languages [4,5,19].

This prior work therefore operates on a higher abstraction level and can thus not reason about architecture-specific details (*e.g.* instruction clock cycles) during the analysis. By building dynamic software analysis tools on an abstract ISA model, we can bridge the gap between the two approaches; we can operate directly on the machine code level while still making it easy to extend the analysis to additional instructions or architectures. This is especially important for modular ISAs like RISC-V.

7   Discussion and Future Work

So far, we have only applied our approach to the RISC-V architecture. Nonetheless, we believe the concepts described in Subsect. 3.2 to be applicable to other

---

[9] https://hackage.haskell.org/package/mtl.

architectures as well. We have, focused on the RISC-V architecture due to its simplicity as we consider the main contribution of this paper to be the implementation of custom interpreters on top of a formal ISA model. A possible direction for future work would be focusing more on modelling aspects by supporting additional RISC-V extensions (especially from the privileged specification [16]), further RISC-V variants (e.g. 64- and 128-bit RISC-V), and maybe even additional ISAs (*e.g.* ARM). Alternatively, it would also be possible to perform further experiments with additional interpreters for our abstract ISA model. We are specifically interested in complementing our own prior work on symbolic execution of RISC-V machine code by implementing it on top of the formal ISA model proposed here, thereby making it easier to extend this prior work to additional RISC-V extension or even additional architectures [26]. More broadly, one end goal of our work in this regard would be facilitating formal ISA models for the implementation of binary software analysis tools along the lines sketched in Subsect. 6.3. Compared to the prevailing prior work on binary software analysis tools—which lifts machine code to an intermediate representation—we believe that building these tools on top of a formal ISA model also allows easier proofs of their correctness. An interesting direction for future work would therefore be investigating the issue of correctness of custom ISA interpreter. As illustrated in Fig. 2, correctness proofs are paramount as we need to ensure that both the abstract and the actual semantics correctly implement the behaviour mandated by the modelled ISA. Considering that our approach is specifically designed to support multiple actual semantics—through custom interpreters—manual validation is infeasible. Instead, it may be possible to leverage existing proof-assistant definitions for ISAs [1] to prove the correctness of created ISA interpreters through computer-aided theorem proving.

8   Conclusion

We have presented a flexible approach for creating functional formal models of instruction set architectures. The functional paradigm gives a natural and concise way to model the instruction format on different levels of abstraction, and the structuring mechanisms allow us to relate these levels. This way, by leveraging free monads, our approach separates instruction semantics from instruction execution. Contrary to prior work, our approach does not make any assumption about the representation of memory/register values. Therefore, it can be used to implement software analysis techniques such as dynamic information flow tracking or symbolic execution; achieving the benefits outlined in Sect. 1.

We have demonstrated our approach by creating an abstract formal model of the RISC-V architecture. Based on this formal RISC-V model, we have created a concrete interpreter—which passes the official RISC-V ISA tests—for the 32-bit base instruction set and a custom interpreter for information flow tracking as a case study. An evaluation conducted with the Embench benchmark suite indicates that our concrete interpreter is faster than prior executable Haskell models of the RISC-V architecture. In future work, we would like to model additional extensions of the RISC-V architecture, perform further experiments with additional interpreters for our model, and investigate correctness proofs for these interpreters through computer-aided theorem proving. To stimulate further research in this direction, we have released our formal RISC-V model as open source software on GitHub.

A   Free Monads and Extensible Effects

Subsection 2.2 introduced the *free monad* for a type constructor f as the closure of f under application, conceptually given as

```
data Free f a = Pure a | Free (f (Free f a))
```

However, this implementation incurs a severe performance penalty. In this appendix, we explain how the library that we use[10] remedies these deficiencies.

The problem is that each application of the functor f corresponds to one application of the constructor Free, and moreover, when running the computation we need to compose from the inside (from the right), whereas we construct monads from the outside (left):

```
run :: (Monad m, Functor f) ⇒ (f (m a) → m a) → Free f a → m a
run _ (Pure x) = pure x
run p (Free f) = p (fmap (run p) f)
```

This makes the run-time of the simple approach quadratic. Kiselyov et al. [9,10] extended the approach, by representing each application of f with a continuation:

```
data Freer f a where
  Pure :: a → Freer f a
  Impure :: f x → (x → Freer a f) → Freer f a
```

This is a generalized algebraic data type (GADT); it is needed here (as opposed to a plain recursive data type) because the argument type a changes in the continuation (the first argument of Impure)[11]. The resulting free monad can be implemented more efficiently, by concatenating all the continuations in a queue, which gives a linear run-time [9].

The data type Freer is not fully *extensible*: once the type variable f is fixed, we cannot later extend it (by adding new types for computations). In our case, this means we have to foresee all possible interpretations in our interpretation of the ISA, or alternatively change the implementation. This limitation can be overcome by combining the free monad with *extensible effects* (see also [27]). Effects insert labels, which are evaluated later, for computational features; they can be made extensible by using an open union type (a type Union r v with injection function inj :: t v→ Union r v and partial projection prj :: Union r v→Maybe (t v)) as labelling type. Crucially, this union type can be extended

---

[10] The aforementioned freer-simple library.
[11] The same effect can be achieved by an existential type variable for x.

at run-time, so we can add effects to our analysis functions later on as we need them; *e.g.* we can adapt the way in which we evaluate expressions, using symbolic evaluation instead of fixed operations on bit-vectors.

Thus, `freer-simple` uses `Union r v` as the functor type, and a second type `Arrs` encapsulates the type-indexed queues:

```
data Eff r a where
  Pure  :: a → Eff r a
  Impure :: Union r x → Arrs r x a → Eff r a
```

This representation is both efficient and extensible, making it flexible as required.

References

1. Armstrong, A., et al.: ISA semantics for ARMv8-a, RISC-V, and CHERI-MIPS. Proc. ACM Program. Lang. **3**(POPL), 1–31 (2019). https://doi.org/10.1145/3290384
2. Baldoni, R., Coppa, E., D'elia, D.C., Demetrescu, C., Finocchi, I.: A survey of symbolic execution techniques. ACM Comput. Surv. **51**(3) (2018). https://doi.org/10.1145/3182657
3. Bluespec Inc.: Forvis: a formal RISC-V ISA specification. GitHub. https://github.com/rsnikhil/Forvis_RISCV-ISA-Spec. Accessed 06 Dec 2022
4. Brumley, David, Jager, Ivan, Avgerinos, Thanassis, Schwartz, Edward J..: BAP: a binary analysis platform. In: Gopalakrishnan, Ganesh, Qadeer, Shaz (eds.) CAV 2011. LNCS, vol. 6806, pp. 463–469. Springer, Heidelberg (2011). https://doi.org/10.1007/978-3-642-22110-1_37
5. Chipounov, V., Kuznetsov, V., Candea, G.: S2E: a platform for in-vivo multi-path analysis of software systems. In: Proceedings of the 16th International Conference on Architectural Support for Programming Languages and Operating Systems, ASPLOS XVI, pp. 265–278. Association for Computing Machinery, New York (2011). https://doi.org/10.1145/1950365.1950396
6. Free and Open Source Silicon Foundation: Embench: a modern embedded benchmark suite. https://www.embench.org/. Accessed 24 Jan 2023
7. Herdt, V., Große, D., Pieper, P., Drechsler, R.: RISC-V based virtual prototype: An extensible and configurable platform for the system-level. J. Syst. Archit. **109**, 101756 (2020). https://doi.org/10.1016/j.sysarc.2020.101756
8. Kelly, G.M.: A unified treatment of transfinite constructions for free algebras, free monoids, colimits, associated sheaves, and so on. Bull. Aust. Math. Soc. **22**(1), 1–83 (1980). https://doi.org/10.1017/S0004972700006353
9. Kiselyov, O., Ishii, H.: Freer monads, more extensible effects. SIGPLAN Not. **50**(12), 94–105 (2015). https://doi.org/10.1145/2887747.2804319
10. Kiselyov, O., Sabry, A., Swords, C.: Extensible effects an alternative to monad transformers. In: Proceedings of the 2013 ACM SIGPLAN Symposium on Haskell, vol. 48, pp. 59–70, January 2014. https://doi.org/10.1145/2578854.2503791
11. Liang, S., Hudak, P., Jones, M.: Monad transformers and modular interpreters. In: Proceedings of the 22nd ACM SIGPLAN-SIGACT Symposium on Principles of Programming Languages, POPL 1995, pp. 333–343. Association for Computing Machinery, New York (1995). https://doi.org/10.1145/199448.199528
12. Massachusetts Institute of Technology: riscv-semantics. GitHub. https://github.com/mit-plv/riscv-semantics. Accessed 06 Dec 2022

13. Pieper, P., Herdt, V., Große, D., Drechsler, R.: Dynamic information flow tracking for embedded binaries using SystemC-based virtual prototypes. In: 2020 57th ACM/IEEE Design Automation Conference (DAC), pp. 1–6 (2020). https://doi.org/10.1109/DAC18072.2020.9218494

14. RISC-V Foundation: ISA Formal Spec Public Review. GitHub (2019). https://github.com/riscvarchive/ISA_Formal_Spec_Public_Review. Accessed 06 Dec 2022

15. RISC-V Foundation: The RISC-V Instruction Set Manual, Volume I: User-Level ISA, December 2019. https://github.com/riscv/riscv-isa-manual/releases/download/Ratified-IMAFDQC/riscv-spec-20191213.pdf. Document Version 20191213

16. RISC-V Foundation: The RISC-V Instruction Set Manual, Volume II: Privileged Architecture, June 2019. https://github.com/riscv/riscv-isa-manual/releases/download/Ratified-IMFDQC-and-Priv-v1.11/riscv-privileged-20190608.pdf. Document Version 20190608-Priv-MSU-Ratified

17. Selfridge, B.: GRIFT: a richly-typed, deeply-embedded RISC-V semantics written in Haskell. In: Workshop on Instruction Set Architecture Specification, SpISA 2019, September 2019. https://www.cl.cam.ac.uk/~jrh13/spisa19/paper_10.pdf

18. Sergey, I., et al.: Monadic abstract interpreters. In: Proceedings of the 34th ACM SIGPLAN Conference on Programming Language Design and Implementation, PLDI 2013, pp. 399–410. Association for Computing Machinery, New York, June 2013. https://doi.org/10.1145/2491956.2491979

19. Shoshitaishvili, Y., et al.: SOK: (state of) the art of war: offensive techniques in binary analysis. In: 2016 IEEE Symposium on Security and Privacy (SP), pp. 138–157 (2016). https://doi.org/10.1109/SP.2016.17

20. Stallings, W.: Computer Organization and Architecture: Designing for Performance, 9th edn. Pearson Education Inc. (2012)

21. Suh, G.E., Lee, J.W., Zhang, D., Devadas, S.: Secure program execution via dynamic information flow tracking. In: Proceedings of the 11th International Conference on Architectural Support for Programming Languages and Operating Systems, ASPLOS XI, pp. 85–96. Association for Computing Machinery, New York (2004). https://doi.org/10.1145/1024393.1024404

22. Swierstra, W.: Data types à la carte. J. Funct. Program. **18**(4), 423–436 (2008). https://doi.org/10.1017/S0956796808006758

23. System C Standardization Working Group: IEEE Standard for Standard SystemC Language Reference Manual. Technical report. IEEE (2012). https://doi.org/10.1109/IEEESTD.2012.6134619

24. Tempel, S., Brandt, T., Lüth, C.: Artifacts for the 2023 trends in functional programming publication: versatile and flexible modelling of the RISC-V instruction set architecture. Zenodo (2023). https://doi.org/10.5281/zenodo.7817414

25. Tempel, S., Herdt, V., Drechsler, R.: Automated detection of spatial memory safety violations for constrained devices. In: Proceedings of the 27th Asia and South Pacific Design Automation Conference, ASPDAC 2022 (2022). https://doi.org/10.1109/ASP-DAC52403.2022.9712570

26. Tempel, S., Herdt, V., Drechsler, R.: SymEx-VP: an open source virtual prototype for OS-agnostic concolic testing of IoT firmware. J. Syst. Archit., 12 (2022). https://doi.org/10.1016/j.sysarc.2022.102456

27. Wadler, P., Thiemann, P.: The marriage of effects and monads. ACM Trans. Comput. Log. 4(1), 1–32 (2003). https://doi.org/10.1145/601775.601776

Faster, Simpler Red-Black Trees

Cameron Moy[✉][iD]

PLT, Northeastern University, Boston, MA 02115, USA
camoy@ccs.neu.edu

Abstract. For more than two decades, functional programmers have refined the persistent red-black tree—a data structure of unrivaled elegance. This paper presents another step in its evolution. Using a monad to communicate balancing information yields a fast insertion procedure, without sacrificing clarity. Employing the same monad plus a new decomposition simplifies the deletion procedure, without sacrificing efficiency.

Keywords: Algorithms · Data Structures · Trees

1 A Quick Recap

A red-black tree is a *self-balancing* binary search tree [3,8]. Insertion and deletion operations rebalance the tree so it never becomes too lopsided. To this end, every node carries an extra bit that "colors" it either red or black. In Haskell [12]:

```
data Color = Red | Black
data Tree a = E | N Color (Tree a) a (Tree a)
```

For convenience, nodes of each color can be constructed and matched using the pattern synonym extension of the Glasgow Haskell Compiler:

```
pattern R a x b = N Red a x b
pattern B a x b = N Black a x b
```

Insertion and deletion use chromatic information to maintain two invariants:

1. The **red-child invariant** states that a red node may not have a red child.
2. The **black-height invariant** states that the number of black nodes along all paths through the tree—the *black height*—is the same.

These two properties imply that the tree is roughly balanced. Naively inserting or deleting nodes from the tree may violate these invariants. Hence, the challenge of implementing red-black trees is to repair the invariants during a modification.

This paper improves on existing work with four contributions: (1) a faster way to implement insertion by avoiding redundant pattern matching; (2) a simpler way to implement deletion by employing two new auxiliary operations; (3) a monad instance that communicates information across recursive calls; (4) an evaluation that compares the performance of several red-black tree implementations. The algorithms are presented in Haskell since it provides a convenient notation for monads, but the approach is not language specific. Appendix A provides a Racket version.

S. Chang (Ed.): TFP 2023, LNCS 13868, pp. 36–50, 2023.
https://doi.org/10.1007/978-3-031-38938-2_3

2   Insertion à la Okasaki

Recall the insertion algorithm of Okasaki [11]. For an ordinary binary search tree, insertion traverses the tree and replaces a leaf with the desired value. For a red-black tree, insertion's first step is the same, with the new node colored red:[1]

Doing so does not introduce a black-height violation but it may introduce a red-child violation if the leaf's parent happens to be red. A **balance** function resolves such red-child violations. A violation can only come in one of four shapes

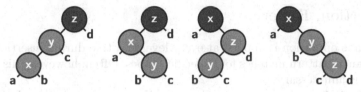

and **balance** fixes the violation by transforming each into:

Realizing this diagram as code is a straightforward, if tedious, exercise:

```
-- Pre: Child may have a red-child violation.
-- Post: Satisfies the red-child invariant;
--       BH(out) = BH(in).²
balance :: Tree a -> Tree a
balance (B (R (R a x b) y c) z d) = R (B a x b) y (B c z d)
balance (B (R a x (R b y c)) z d) = R (B a x b) y (B c z d)
balance (B a x (R (R b y c) z d)) = R (B a x b) y (B c z d)
balance (B a x (R b y (R c z d))) = R (B a x b) y (B c z d)
balance s = s
```

Since **balance** can turn a black node into a red node, this may induce a red-child violation one level up the tree. Thus, **insert** must **balance** at every level. This process "bubbles" violations up the tree. At the end, **insert** blackens the root to resolve the last possible violation:

---

[1] The diagrams use the letters x, y, z for values; the letters a, b, c, d for subtrees; and • for the empty tree.

[2] Where BH computes the black height of a tree.

```
insert :: Ord a => a -> Tree a -> Tree a
insert x s = (blacken . ins) s
  where ins E = R E x E
        ins (N k a y b)
             | x <  y = balance (N k (ins a) y b)
             | x == y = N k a y b
             | x >  y = balance (N k a y (ins b))

blacken :: Tree a -> Tree a
blacken (N _ a y b) = B a y b
blacken s = s
```

3 Insertion, Faster

The **balance** operation is applied at every level of a tree during insertion. Each time, **balance** pattern matches four specific shapes. Often, however, this pattern matching is unnecessary.

Suppose **balance** returns a black node. No more red-child violations can occur further up the tree, since the rest of the tree satisfies the red-child invariant. In other words, when **balance** produces a black node, the "bubbling" stops. No more work needs to be done and every subsequent **balance** is redundant.

For a mutable data structure, a **break** statement could eliminate the extra work. For an immutable data structure, a different solution is needed. An additional data type[3] makes short circuiting future operations possible:

```
type Result a = Result' a a
data Result' a b = D a | T b
```

A **Result** contains a tree where either the work is *done*, constructed with D, or there is more *to do*, constructed with T. Trees marked with D do not violate the red-child invariant, while trees marked with T may. Trees marked with D can pass forward unaffected, while trees marked with T must be fixed by calling **balance**.

A **Monad** instance for **Result** makes this use case easy to express. A tree where more work needs to be done is given to a function **f**, while a tree that is done propagates:

```
instance Monad (Result' a) where
  return x = T x
  (D x) >>= f = D x
  (T x) >>= f = f x
```

Two functions on **Result** values prove useful too. The **fromResult** function extracts trees from a **Result**

```
fromResult (D x) = x
fromResult (T x) = x
```

---

[3] This type is the same as **Either**, but with more convenient constructors.

and <$$> applies a function to the contents of both T and D values[4]

```
f <$$> (D x) = D (f x)
f <$$> (T x) = T (f x)
```

Equipped with `Result`, suspended calls to `balance` further up a tree can be bypassed by wrapping a subtree in D. As mentioned before, it is safe to do so whenever `balance` produces a black node. Here is the new `balance` function:

```
balance :: Tree a -> Result (Tree a)
balance (B (R (R a x b) y c) z d) = T (R (B a x b) y (B c z d))
balance (B (R a x (R b y c)) z d) = T (R (B a x b) y (B c z d))
balance (B a x (R (R b y c) z d)) = T (R (B a x b) y (B c z d))
balance (B a x (R b y (R c z d))) = T (R (B a x b) y (B c z d))
balance (B a x b) = D (B a x b)
balance (R a x b) = T (R a x b)
```

Now that `balance` returns a `Result` value, `insert` must handle it. The essence of the function, however, remains the same:

```
insert :: Ord a => a -> Tree a -> Tree a
insert x s = (blacken . fromResult . ins) s
  where ins E = T (R E x E)
        ins (N k a y b)
          | x <  y = balance =<< (\a -> N k a y b) <$$> ins a
          | x == y = D (N k a y b)
          | x >  y = balance =<< (\b -> N k a y b) <$$> ins b
```

Using this approach, insertion can be up to 1.56× faster than the original one.

4 Deletion, Simpler

As with `insert`, the `delete` function is similar to ordinary deletion on a binary search tree. For an internal node, `delete` replaces the target node with its in-order successor. Only the base cases, where no in-order successor exists, are interesting. The following diagram shows all three:

Deleting a red node does not introduce a black-height violation, but deleting a black node might if its left child is empty; an empty left child provides no opportunity to maintain the black height. In other words, the subtree becomes *short* with respect to black height.

---

[4] Note that <$$> is not `fmap`. The functor instance implied by the monad applies a function only to T values.

Two auxiliary functions are needed to repair short subtrees: `balance'` and `eq`. Like `balance`, the `balance'` function resolves red-child violations. Unlike `balance`, it simultaneously increases a tree's black height. The `eq` function takes a tree where one child is short and equalizes the children's black heights. Both auxiliary functions use `Result` to communicate shortness information. Here, `Result` has a slightly different interpretation than `Result` for `insert`.

Recall that `insert` always adds a red node, *possibly* causing a red-child violation. Subtrees are wrapped in `T` if there *might* be a violation and `D` if there is not. In contrast, the final base case for `delete` *always* causes a black-height violation. Thus, a subtree is wrapped in `T` if it is *definitely* short and `D` otherwise.

4.1 `balance'`

The purpose of `balance'` is to resolve red-child violations and, if possible, increase the black height by one. To accomplish this, the function acts like `balance`, except the root color is preserved. So the following four shapes[5]

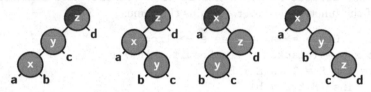

are transformed into

Whether the root is black or red, all red-child violations are resolved and the black height is increased by one. If none of the four shapes match, then the tree is blackened. Differences compared to `balance` are highlighted:

```
-- Pre: Root or child may have a red-child violation.
-- Post: Satisfies the red-child invariant;
--       BH(out) = BH(in) + 1 or BH(out) = BH(in).
balance' :: Tree a -> Result (Tree a)
balance' (N k (R (R a x b) y c) z d) = D (N k (B a x b) y (B c z d))
balance' (N k (R a x (R b y c)) z d) = D (N k (B a x b) y (B c z d))
balance' (N k a x (R (R b y c) z d)) = D (N k (B a x b) y (B c z d))
balance' (N k a x (R b y (R c z d))) = D (N k (B a x b) y (B c z d))
balance' s = blacken' s

blacken' :: Tree a -> Tree a
blacken' (R a y b) = D (B a y b)
blacken' s = T s
```

---

[5] The half-colored nodes indicate that the color could be either red or black.

Three facts are worth noting. First, not only can **balance'** resolve trees with two red nodes in a row, but also trees where there are three red nodes in a row. Second, **balance'** never induces a red-child violation further up the tree because it never turns a black node into a red node. Finally, when provided a red node, **balance'** always returns a D result.

4.2   eq

Just as **insert** needs **balance**, **delete** needs a function that can repair the black-height invariant at every level of the tree. That is the purpose of **eq**. Although it is possible to define a single function to get the job done, it is convenient to split the function in two: **eqL** and **eqR**.[6]

Given a short left (right) child, **eqL** (**eqR**) returns a tree where the black heights of the children are equal. If the function can raise the black height of the left (right) child, it does so. If it cannot, it lowers the black height of the sibling and bubbles the violation up.

Consider **eqL**, where the left child, labeled **a**, is short. There are two cases to consider: when its sibling is black and when its sibling is red. Here is the first case, where the sibling is black and the root is any color:[7]

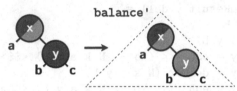

To equalize the black heights, **eqL** reduces the black height of the right child by reddening it. Now the whole tree is short. Not only that, but this can introduce red-child violations. If **b** is red, there may even be three red nodes in a row. The **balance'** function is designed to handle all of these issues simultaneously:

```
-- Pre: BH(left) = BH(right) - 1.
-- Post: BH(left) = BH(right).
eqL :: Tree a -> Result (Tree a)
eqL (N k a y (B c z d)) = balance' (N k a y (R c z d))

-- Pre: BH(right) = BH(left) - 1.
-- Post: BH(right) = BH(left).
eqR :: Tree a -> Result (Tree a)
eqR (N k (B a x b) y c) = balance' (N k (R a x b) y c)
```

Next, consider the case where the sibling is red. Here, **eqL** applies a rotation that does not affect any black heights and calls itself recursively on the left child:

---

[6] Some split **balance** into **balanceL** and **balanceR** [10, exercise 3.10]. For **balance**, splitting is done for performance rather than convenience.

[7] The dotted triangle encloses the tree that **balance'** is applied to.

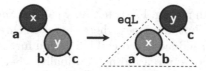

After the rotation, **a** is still short and the other subtrees are unchanged. However, as noted before, `balance'` resolves a black-height violation when called on a red node. Thus, it is guaranteed that the recursive call to `eqL` successfully increases the black height of **a**, yielding a valid red-black tree:

```
eqL (N k a y (R c z d)) = (\a -> B a z d) <$$> eqL (R a y c)
eqR (N k (R a x b) y c) = (\b -> B a x b) <$$> eqR (R b y c)
```

4.3   Putting It Together

Here is the rest of the code, which composes the presented functions into a complete algorithm:

```
delete :: Ord a => a -> Tree a -> Tree a
delete x s = (fromResult . del) s
  where del E = D E
        del (N k a y b)
          | x <  y = eqL =<< (\a -> N k a y b) <$$> del a
          | x == y = delCur (N k a y b)
          | x >  y = eqR =<< (\b -> N k a y b) <$$> del b


delCur :: Tree a -> Result (Tree a)
delCur (R a y E)   = D a
delCur (B a y E)   = blacken' a
delCur (N k a y b) = eqR =<< (\b -> N k a min b) <$$> b'
   where (b', min) = delMin b


delMin :: Tree a -> (Result (Tree a), a)
delMin (R E y b)   = (D b, y)
delMin (B E y b)   = (blacken' b, y)
delMin (N k a y b) = (eqL =<< (\a -> N k a y b) <$$> a', min)
   where (a', min) = delMin a
```

5   Performance Evaluation

Using monads to communicate balancing information yields a unified and elegant presentation of both insertion and deletion; critically though, these variants perform as well as or better than existing algorithms. The next two pages summarize a performance evaluation for several functional red-black tree algorithms.

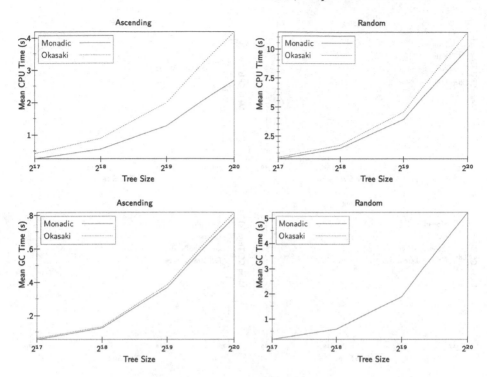

Fig. 1. Insertion Line Plots

Table 1. Insertion Measurements (Mean ± Standard Deviation)

Benchmark	Algorithm	CPU (s)	GC (s)	Memory (MB)
ASCENDING (2^{20})	Monadic	2.68 ± 0.01	0.79 ± 0.01	7807 ± 1
	Okasaki	4.19 ± 0.01	0.82 ± 0.01	7810 ± 1
RANDOM (2^{20})	Monadic	10 ± 0.07	5.21 ± 0.03	5619 ± 7
	Okasaki	11.43 ± 0.1	5.22 ± 0.05	5622 ± 8
SUFFIXTREE	Monadic	4.99 ± 0.05	0.33 ± 0.01	2720 ± 1
	Okasaki	5.35 ± 0.03	0.33 ± 0.01	2720 ± 1

Figure 1 and Table 1 present the data for insertion. Figure 2 and Table 2 present the data for deletion.

These measurements were collected on a Linux machine running an Intel Xeon E3 processor at 3.10 GHz with 32 GB of RAM. Since the different algorithms were originally implemented in different languages, they were all ported to Racket [5] and run with Racket 8.7 CS. Racket is a strict language, so the performance characteristics should generalize better than that of a lazy language like Haskell. Every sample ran the entire sequence of operations 5 times and 100 such samples were collected for each configuration.

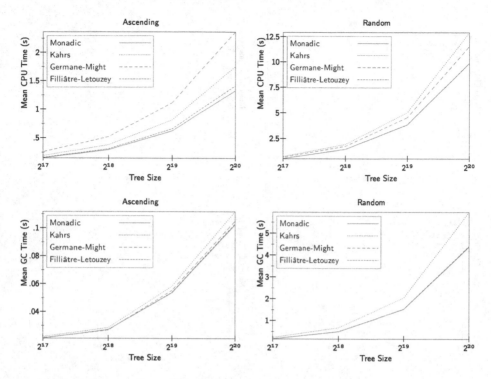

Fig. 2. Deletion Line Plots

Table 2. Deletion Measurements (Mean ± Standard Deviation)

Benchmark	Algorithm	CPU (s)	GC (s)	Memory (MB)
ASCENDING (2^{20})	Monadic	1.32 ± 0.01	0.1 ± 0	4685 ± 34
	Kahrs	1.75 ± 0.02	0.11 ± 0	7324 ± 58
	Germane-Might	2.36 ± 0.03	0.1 ± 0	5377 ± 64
	Filliâtre-Letouzey	1.41 ± 0.01	0.1 ± 0	4918 ± 33
RANDOM (2^{20})	Monadic	9.88 ± 0.11	4.38 ± 0.03	5376 ± 15
	Kahrs	12.93 ± 0.13	5.96 ± 0.03	8635 ± 32
	Germane-Might	11.56 ± 0.13	4.39 ± 0.04	5301 ± 11
	Filliâtre-Letouzey	9.9 ± 0.1	4.41 ± 0.02	5328 ± 11

A configuration consists of a specific choice for input size, input order, and algorithm. For a given size n, the input values are the first n natural numbers, ordered in two different ways: ascending and random. The random order is a random permutation of the input data.

To test insertion and deletion, each red-black tree algorithm was used to implement sets. Insertion was tested by adding all the input values to an empty set. Deletion was tested by removing all the input values from a set containing them already.

As an additional benchmark for insertion, the SUFFIXTREE program from the gradual typing benchmark suite [7] was adapted to use red-black trees instead of hash tables. This program uses Ukkonen's algorithm to calculate the suffix tree of a text—in this case T.S. Eliot's "Prufrock."

The line plots in Fig. 1 and Fig. 2 show mean execution time, both total execution time including garbage collection (GC) and just GC time, across several tree sizes. Note that the plots are log scale. Table 1 and Table 2 give the mean and standard deviation of total execution time, GC time, and memory consumption for the same benchmarks.

Monadic insertion is about 1.14× faster than Okasaki's original [11] when inserting 2^{20} elements in a random order. When the input sequence is in ascending order, this improvement increases to about 1.56× faster. On the SUFFIXTREE benchmark it is 1.07× faster, demonstrating that the optimization has a measurable impact on the end-to-end performance of a real-world program.

Monadic deletion performs the same, or a tad better, than the algorithm of Filliâtre and Letouzey [4], currently the best known approach. On a randomly distributed deletion sequence, their performance exactly coincides. The monadic approach is significantly faster than that of Kahrs [9] and Germane and Might [6]. This evaluation demonstrates that the simplicity of the monadic deletion algorithm does not come at the cost of performance.

6   Related Work

Okasaki [11] gave a beautiful account of insertion, but omitted any discussion of deletion. Deletion is more difficult than insertion because black-height invariance is a global property; whether a subtree violates the black-height invariant can be determined only through inspection of the entire tree. To avoid this, a subtree must somehow indicate that its black height is too small—that it is short. Every paper on red-black trees does this differently.

Filliâtre and Letouzey [4] develop an implementation where shortness is handled in an ad-hoc way using a threaded Boolean. Germane and Might [6] use a "double-black" color to serve the same function. The `Result` monad has the same purpose, but eliminates the manual bookkeeping necessary in both of them. Kahrs [9] describes a significantly different approach; it maintains an additional invariant during the deletion process: black nodes are always short and red nodes are never short. Thus, the information is communicated implicitly rather than explicitly.

The deletion algorithm presented here is substantially simpler to understand than prior work for two reasons. First, all prior algorithms have three cases for `eq` instead of just two. By factoring out `balance'`, two special cases collapse into one. Second, all prior algorithms require contortions to deal with the red sibling case. Specifically, each uses a three-level pattern match combined with a nested `balance` operation. The `eq` function presented here uses a two-level pattern match and recursion instead.

Germane and Might report that their double-black algorithm has poor performance—substantially worse than the one given by Kahrs. However, their evaluation is fatally flawed; it measures a version of the double-black algorithm with a suboptimal order of conditional branches. Reordering these branches improves performance. Section 5 evaluates a corrected variant of Germane and Might's code. See Appendix B for an explanation of this modification.

A related line of work focuses on proving the correctness of red-black tree algorithms using proof assistants [1,4] and GADTs [9,13]. These techniques should easily be applicable to this paper, and doing so is left as an exercise to the reader.

7   Conclusion

Given the beauty of red-black tree insertion, the absence of a deletion algorithm that is simultaneously efficient and simple has been unfortunate. Using the `Result` monad yields an algorithm that, along with `balance'` and `eq`, achieves both goals. The same monadic style can be applied to insertion, yielding a faster algorithm, without compromising simplicity.

Acknowledgements. Thanks to Matthias Felleisen for his feedback and encouragement. Also, thanks to Ben Lerner, Jason Hemann, Leif Andersen, Michael Ballantyne, Mitch Gamburg, Sam Caldwell, audience members at TFP, and anonymous TFP reviewers for providing valuable comments that significantly improved the exposition.

Much of the code in this paper was directly adapted or at least heavily influenced by the code of Okasaki [11] (for insertion) and Germane and Might [6] (for deletion). They deserve a great deal of credit for the final product.

This work was partially supported by NSF grant SHF 2116372.

A   Racket Implementation

This section shows a Racket port of the Haskell code. Monads can be implemented in many ways, but the following code uses macros and multiple return values [2] to do so. This choice yields excellent performance.

```
;;;;;;;;;;;;;;;;;;;;;;;;;;;;;;;;;;;;;;;;;;
;; insert

(define (insert t x)
  (define (ins t)
    (match t
      [(E) (todo (R (E) x (E)))]
      [(N k a y b)
       (cond
         [(< x y) (=<< balance (<$$> (λ (a) (N k a y b)) (ins a)))]
         [(> x y) (=<< balance (<$$> (λ (b) (N k a y b)) (ins b)))]
         [else    (done t)])]))
```

```
      (blacken (from-result (ins t))))

(define (balance t)
  (match t
    [(or (B (R a x (R b y c)) z d)
         (B (R (R a x b) y c) z d)
         (B a x (R (R b y c) z d))
         (B a x (R b y (R c z d))))
     (todo (R (B a x b) y (B c z d)))]
    [(B _ _ _) (done t)]
    [_         (todo t)]))

(define (blacken t)
  (match t
    [(R a x b) (B a x b)]
    [_         t]))

;;;;;;;;;;;;;;;;;;;;;;;;;;;;;;;;;;;;;;;;;;
;; delete

(define (delete t x)
  (define (del t)
    (match-define (N k a y b) t)
    (cond
      [(< x y) (=<< del-left  (<$$> (λ (a) (N k a y b)) (del a)))]
      [(> x y) (=<< del-right (<$$> (λ (b) (N k a y b)) (del b)))]
      [else    (del-root t)]))
  (from-result (del t)))

(define (del-root t)
  (match t
    [(B a y (E)) (blacken* a)]
    [(R a y (E)) (done a)]
    [(N k a y b)
     (define m (box false))
     (=<< del-right (<$$> (λ (b) (N k a (unbox m) b)) (del-min b m)))]))

(define (del-min t m)
  (match t
    [(B (E) y b) (set-box! m y) (blacken* b)]
    [(R (E) y b) (set-box! m y) (done b)]
    [(N k a y b)
     (=<< del-left (<$$> (λ (a) (N k a y b)) (del-min a m)))]))

(define (del-left t)
  (match t
    [(N k a y (R c z d))
     (<$$> (λ (a) (B a z d)) (del-left (R a y c)))]
    [(N k a y (B c z d))
     (balance* (N k a y (R c z d)))]))
```

```
(define (del-right t)
  (match t
    [(N k (R a x b) y c)
     (<$$> (λ (b) (B a x b)) (del-right (R b y c)))]
    [(N k (B a x b) y c)
     (balance* (N k (R a x b) y c))]))

(define (balance* t)
  (match t
    [(or (N k (R a x (R b y c)) z d)
         (N k (R (R a x b) y c) z d)
         (N k a x (R (R b y c) z d))
         (N k a x (R b y (R c z d))))
     (done (N k (B a x b) y (B c z d)))]
    [_ (blacken* t)]))

(define (blacken* t)
  (match t
    [(R a x b) (done (B a x b))]
    [_         (todo t)]))

;;;;;;;;;;;;;;;;;;;;;;;;;;;;;;;;;;;;;;;;
;; monad

(define-syntax-rule (todo x)
  (values true x))

(define-syntax-rule (done x)
  (values false x))

(define-syntax-rule (from-result x)
  (let-values ([(_ y) x])
    y))

(define-syntax-rule (<$$> f x)
  (let-values ([(a d) x])
    (values a (f d))))

(define-syntax-rule (=<< f x)
  (let-values ([(ax dx) x])
    (if ax (f dx) (values ax dx))))

;;;;;;;;;;;;;;;;;;;;;;;;;;;;;;;;;;;;;;;;
;; data

(struct E ())
(struct N (color left value right))

(define-syntax-rule (define-color name)
```

```
(begin
  (define-for-syntax (transf stx)
    (syntax-case stx ()
      [(_ a x b) #'(N 'name a x b)]))
  (define-match-expander name transf transf)))

(define-color R)
(define-color B)
```

B   Performance Evaluation Correction

Germane and Might [6] incorrectly conclude that their algorithm is always significantly slower than other approaches. This conclusion is due to a subtle confounding factor that put their algorithm at an unfair disadvantage.

To understand the flaw, consider this skeleton of their `delete` function:

```
delete :: Ord a => a -> Tree a -> Tree a
delete x s = del (redden s)
  where del E = E
        del (R E y E)
          | x == y = ...
          | x /= y = ...
        del (B E y E)
          | x == y = ...
          | x /= y = ...
        del (B (R E y E) z E)
          | x < z  = ...
          | x == z = ...
          | x > z  = ...
        del (N k a y b)
          | x < y  = ...
          | x == y = ...
          | x > y  = ...
```

It highlights the two most common cases during deletion, when the current node does not match the target and the function recurs on either the left or right side. However, the structure of the code forces each of the base cases to be checked first—before the most common cases.

To favor the common cases, the skeleton should look as follows:

```
delete :: Ord a => a -> Tree a -> Tree a
delete x s = del (redden s)
  where del E = E
        del (N k a y b)
          | x < y  = ...
          | x == y =
```

```
case s of
  R E y E -> ...
  B E y E -> ...
  B (R E y E) z E -> ...
| x > y = ...
```

The base cases are only checked at the target node. This simple modification improves the performance of the double-black algorithm by 2×.

References

1. Appel, A.: Efficient verified red-black trees (2011). https://www.cs.princeton.edu/~appel/papers/redblack.pdf
2. Ashley, J.M., Dybvig, R.K.: An efficient implementation of multiple return values in scheme. In: LISP and Functional Programming (LFP) (1994). https://doi.org/10.1145/182590.156784
3. Cormen, T., Leiserson, C., Rivest, R., Stein, C.: Introduction to Algorithms. MIT Press (2009)
4. Filliâtre, J.-C., Letouzey, P.: Functors for proofs and programs. In: Schmidt, D. (ed.) ESOP 2004. LNCS, vol. 2986, pp. 370–384. Springer, Heidelberg (2004). https://doi.org/10.1007/978-3-540-24725-8_26
5. Flatt, M., PLT: reference: racket. Technical report. PLT-TR-2010-1, PLT Design Inc. (2010). https://racket-lang.org/tr1/
6. Germane, K., Might, M.: Deletion: the curse of the red-black tree. J. Funct. Program. (JFP) (2014). https://doi.org/10.1017/S0956796814000227
7. Greenman, B., et al.: How to evaluate the performance of gradual typing systems. J. Funct. Program. (JFP) (2019). https://doi.org/10.1017/S0956796818000217
8. Guibas, L., Sedgewick, R.: A dichromatic framework for balanced trees. In: IEEE Symposium on Foundations of Computer Science (1978). https://doi.org/10.1109/SFCS.1978.3
9. Kahrs, S.: Red-black trees with types. J. Funct. Program. (JFP) (2001). https://doi.org/10.1017/S0956796801004026
10. Okasaki, C.: Purely Functional Data Structures. Cambridge University Press (1999)
11. Okasaki, C.: Red-black trees in a functional setting. J. Funct. Program. (JFP) (1999). https://doi.org/10.1017/S0956796899003494
12. Peyton Jones, S.: Haskell 98 Language and Libraries: The Revised Report. Cambridge University Press (2003)
13. Weirich, S.: Red black trees (redux) (2021). https://www.seas.upenn.edu/~cis5520/21fa/lectures/stub/06-GADTs/RedBlackGADT0.html

MatchMaker: A DSL for Game-Theoretic Matching

Prashant Kumar[✉][iD] and Martin Erwig[iD]

Oregon State University, Corvallis, OR 97330, USA
{kumarpra,erwig}@oregonstate.edu

Abstract. Existing tools for solving game-theoretic matching problems
are limited in their expressiveness and can be difficult to use. In this
paper, we introduce MATCHMAKER, a Haskell-based domain-specific
embedded language (DSEL), which supports the direct, high-level representation of matching problems. Haskell's type system, particularly the
use of multi-parameter type classes, facilitates the definition of a highly
general interface to matching problems, which can be rapidly instantiated
for a wide variety of different matching applications. Additionally, as a
novel contribution, MATCHMAKER provides combinators for dynamically
updating and modifying problem representations, as well as for analyzing
matching results.

Keywords: DSL · Language Design · Matching Problems

1 Introduction

A large class of problems are instances of matching problems. Examples include
the assignment of children to different schools, students to universities and cam-
pus housing, doctors to hospitals, kidney transplant patients to donors, and
many others. In each of these problems, the participants in the matching process typically have *preferences* over the entities they are matched to, and the
task is to find a matching that is, in some sense, optimal with respect to these
preferences. The importance of matching is also highlighted by the fact that the
2012 Nobel Prize in Economics was awarded to Lloyd S. Shapley and Alvin E.
Roth for their work on stable matching problems.

Despite its apparent usefulness, the actual software support for expressing
and solving matching problems is surprisingly limited in a number of ways. For
example, the currently available software tools for solving matching problems
are limited in expressiveness and often difficult to use. Almost all the available
matching libraries use strings to encode the matching problem, which affects
readability and maintainability of the encoded problems. Employing untyped
representations limits the options for checking the validity of the encoding and
producing meaningful error messages. As we will demonstrate, MATCHMAKER
leverages Haskell's rich type system and its type class system to facilitate high-
level representations of matching problems that are readable, easily modifiable,
and provide good error checking.

S. Chang (Ed.): TFP 2023, LNCS 13868, pp. 51–71, 2023.
https://doi.org/10.1007/978-3-031-38938-2_4

Arthur	Sunny	Joseph	Latha	Darrius
City	City	City	Mercy	City
	Mercy	General	City	Mercy
		Mercy	General	General

(a) Applicants' hospital preferences

Mercy	City	General
Darrius	Darrius	Darrius
Joseph	Arthur	Arthur
	Sunny	Joseph
	Latha	Latha
	Joseph	

(b) Hospitals' ranking of applicants

Fig. 1. Matching hospitals with applicants: a two-sided stable matching example.

MATCHMAKER already implements algorithms for a large class of matching problems. More specifically, we implement *bipartite stable matching with two-sided preferences*, *bipartite stable matching with one-sided preferences*, and *same-set matching problems with one-sided preferences*. Together, these represent the most important and widely applicable matching problems [7,11,17].

Our DSL makes the following main contributions. It:

- offers a high-level, type-safe, extensible representation for matching problems.
- defines a scalable mechanism for describing preferences based on function definitions and abstract criteria.
- provides functions to analyze and compare the results of various matchings.
- is easily extensible to represent new matching problems.

The remainder of this paper is structured as follows. In Sect. 2, we introduce stable bipartite matching problems with two-sided preferences and encode them in MATCHMAKER with explicit preferences. In Sect. 3, we illustrate how to represent preferences implicitly using Haskell's abstract data types and functions. In Sect. 4, we introduce combinators to update the existing matching representations plus functions for comparing the results of two matchings. In Sect. 6, we compare MATCHMAKER to other tools for matching. Finally, in Sect. 7 we provide conclusions.

2 Bipartite Stable Matching with Two-Sided Preferences

Consider the task of assigning medical residency applicants to hospitals. Figure 1 shows an example taken from the National Resident Matching Program's (NRMP) website [12] in which five applicants apply to the three hospitals. Hospitals and applicants list their preferences, and each hospital can accept at most two applicants. The stable matching algorithm (also called *delayed acceptance algorithm* [4,14]) produces a match with the following two characteristics:

(1) Each applicant is assigned to only one hospital, and no hospital is assigned more applicants than its quota.

(2) The resulting match is *stable*.

This stability condition is described in the delayed acceptance algorithm as the match not having a *blocking pair*, which is a pair of a hospital and an applicant currently assigned to different partners but who prefer each other more than their current assignment. The presence of such pairs undermines the effectiveness of the matching process, as these pairs can make private arrangements, leaving behind their partners assigned by the matching algorithm. Roth and Sotomayor show an example of an unstable matching mechanism for matching doctors to hospitals in Birmingham and Newcastle used in the 1960s s and 1970s s [17, Chapter 5]. The instability of the outcome led to doctors and hospitals entering private negotiations outside the matching process, which left many doctors without a position and many hospitals without a resident. This culminated in the abandonment of the mechanism. Gale and Shapley [4] showed that a special property of bipartite matching markets is that stable matchings always exist.

Let us try to match hospitals with applicants, taking into account their preferences and quotas. Consider the preference list of Darrius. He prefers City Hospital the most, and City Hospital also ranks him the highest amongst the candidates. It is easy to deduce that Darrius will end up at City Hospital. Now, if we look at the preference list of Sunny, we see that she considers only City and Mercy for her residency. However, Sunny is not included in Mercy Hospital's rankings, so she cannot be assigned there. Her first option, City Hospital, does rank her third. However, notice that the two people ranked above her, Darrius and Arthur, have listed City as their first choice. If they are assigned the two positions, then Sunny is left without an offer, as Mercy is the only hospital in her preference set that also ranks her.

Could we have accommodated Darrius at Mercy Hospital, leaving room for Sunny at City Hospital? Although this does lead to Sunny getting accommodated at City Hospital, it results in instability in the matching process due to the formation of a blocking pair between Darrius and City Hospital. Darrius still prefers City Hospital to Mercy Hospital, and City Hospital still prefers Darrius to Sunny. In other words, they both benefit from forming their own match, leaving behind their assigned matches.

In this section, we demonstrate how to represent this example in MATCH-MAKER and generate a stable matching. To motivate the different design choices, it is instructive to look at the formal model of stable matching.

2.1   Modeling Stable Matching

A two-sided stable matching problem between applicants and hospitals is a 6 tuple $(A, H, P_A, P_H, Q_A, Q_H)$ where $A = \{a_1, \ldots, a_m\}$ and $H = \{h_1, \ldots, h_n\}$ represent the finite disjoint sets of applicants and hospitals, respectively [17]. The preference of each applicant $a \in A$ is represented by an ordered list of preferences $P(a)$ on set H. Similarly, the preference of each hospital $h \in H$ is represented by an ordered list of preferences $P(h)$ on set A. The set of all preference lists is captured by the functions $P_A : A \to H^*$ and $P_H : H \to A^*$.

```
import qualified Data.Map as M

type Capacity = Int

forall :: Capacity -> a -> Capacity
forall c _ = c

class (Bounded a,Enum a,Ord a) => Set a where
    members :: [a]
    members = enumFromTo minBound maxBound

    quota :: a -> Capacity
    quota = forall 1

data Rec b c   = Rec  {unRec :: M.Map b c}
data Info a b c = Info {unInfo :: M.Map a (Rec b c)}

data Rank = Rank {unRank :: Int}

class Preference a b c | a b -> c where
  gather :: Info a b c

type Ord2 a b = (Ord a, Ord b)
type Preference2 a b c d = (Preference a b c,Preference b a d)

info    :: Ord2 a b => [(a,[(b,c)])] -> Info a b c
choices :: Ord2 a b => [(a,[b])] -> Info a b Rank

data Match a b = Match {unMatch:: [(a,[b], Capacity)]}

ranks :: (Set2 a b,Norm c,Weights a) => Info a b c -> Match a b

twoWay :: (Preference2 a b c d,Set2 a b,Norm2 c d) => Match a b

twoWayWithCapacity :: (Preference2 a b c d,Set2 a b,Norm2 c d) =>  Match a b

twoWayWithPref :: (Preference2 a b c d,Set2 a b,Norm2 c d) => Info a b c ->
                  Info b a d -> Match a b
```

Fig. 2. Definitions for encoding and storing preferences in MATCHMAKER.

Each hospital h is also assigned a positive integer $Q(h)$, also called its *quota*, that represents the maximum number of applicants it could admit. Similarly, each applicant is also assigned a quota. This information is collected in the two functions $Q_A : A \to \mathbb{N}$ and $Q_H : H \to \mathbb{N}$. For the applicant-hospital matching problem, it is obvious that applicants have a quota of 1, since they can work at only one hospital. However, in other examples of matching problems with two-sided preferences, both the sets can have quotas greater than 1.

A *matching* is a relation $\mu \subseteq A \times H$ that satisfies the following two conditions: (1) $\forall a \in A : |\mu(a)| \leq Q_A(a)$ and $\forall h \in H : |\mu(h)| \leq Q_H(h)$ and (2) $(a,h) \in \mu \Rightarrow a \in P(h) \wedge h \in P(a)$. The first condition ensures the matching satisfies the quota restrictions, and the second condition ensures consistency. In our current example that means that a hospital is in an applicant's match only if they are in each other's preference list.

The formal model guides the design of our DSL, which we demonstrate with the help of our example next.

2.2 DSL Representation of Matching Problems

The first step in encoding our example is to represent the two sets to be matched as Haskell data types.

```
data Applicant = Arthur | Sunny | Joseph | Latha | Darrius
data Hospital  = City | Mercy | General
```

The definitions and type signatures of various data types, type classes, and functions used in this section are summarized in Fig. 2.

To store the preferences of the applicants and hospitals we use two mappings: `Rec` and `Info`, which is a collection of `Recs`, represented as a mapping[1]. Specifically, `Info Applicant Hospital Rank` maps every applicant to a record `Rec Hospital Rank`, which maps hospitals to their ranks as specified by the applicant. Similarly, the ranking of applicants by hospitals is represented in `Info Hospital Applicant Rank`, where the individual preferences of each hospital are recorded in the mapping `Rec Hospital Rank`.

We define `Functor` instances of the `Rec` and `Info` types in Fig. 4. We use these instances to define their corresponding `zap` functions (also in Fig. 4), which are useful for creating combinators like `zipInfo` that we later use in the paper.[2] It can be thought of as a generalization of the `zip` function, where instead of just combining two functorial structures (like lists), we can combine any number of functorial structures using corresponding functions.

The multi-parameter type class `Preference a b c` provides an interface for specifying preferences. An interesting aspect of the class definition is the functional dependency specification, which signifies that types `a` and `b` uniquely determine type `c`. The `gather` function of the type class captures the preference of elements of set `a` for elements of set `b` using a type `c` and stores it in the mapping `Info a b c`. The smart constructors `info` and `choices` are used to construct the preference mappings from list of tuples.[3]

To keep the number of class constraints manageable in Fig. 2, we use a Haskell language extension called `ConstraintKinds`, which allows us to define class constraints more succinctly using type synonyms. For instance, instead of using `(Ord a, Ord b)` as the class constraint, we can use its type synonym `Ord2 a b`. We have similar definitions for `Norm2`, `Set2` and `Preference2 a b c d`.

Our current example requires two-sided specification of preferences. This entails two instance definitions of the `Preference` class, one for hospitals and one for applicants. However, before presenting those definitions, we discuss a particular design choice for the type class. One question is whether we should have simplified the definitions of the `Info` mappings and consequently the `Preference` class by removing their last type argument and hard-coding the `Rank` in the definitions instead. This would mean that the rank of an item is specified by the position of that item in a list. While this does simplify the design, the constraint to relate the items being matched in just one way also limits the expressivity of the domain. The advantages of our design choice become apparent in Sect. 3

---

[1] The mappings are represented by the `Data.Map.Map` data type from the standard `containers` package of Haskell.

[2] Thanks to the one of the reviewers for suggesting the use of `zap`.

[3] We mostly show only the type signatures and present implementations only when they contribute to a better understanding. For the complete code, see https://github.com/prashant007/MatchMaker.

where we instantiate the third argument of `Info` and `Preference` with richer types than `Rank` that allow agents to implicitly rank other agents, which eases the cognitive burden and effort in defining preference lists.

The ranked preference lists of applicants for hospitals can be specified with an appropriate instance of `Preference` type class using the `choices` function as shown below. The infix operation `-->` is simply syntactic sugar for building pairs. In this representation, rankings are based on positions. For example, the fact that City precedes Mercy in the preference list of Sunny means that she prefers City to Mercy.

```
instance Preference Applicant Hospital Rank where
  gather = choices [Arthur  --> [City],
                    Sunny   --> [City,Mercy],
                    Joseph  --> [City,General,Mercy],
                    Latha   --> [Mercy,City,General],
                    Darrius --> [City,Mercy,General]]
```

The ranked preference lists of applicants for hospitals can be similarly encoded.

```
instance Preference Hospital Applicant Rank where
  gather = choices [Mercy   --> [Darrius,Joseph],
                    City    --> [Darrius,Arthur,Sunny,Latha,Joseph],
                    General --> [Darrius,Arthur,Joseph,Latha]]
```

Finally, to encode the quota information, we define a type class called `Set` with `quota` as a member function as shown in Fig. 2. We also define a function `members` that can list all the elements of a set. The function `forall` is used to assign the same quota to every member of the set to be matched.

The instances of `Set` for the `Applicant` and the `Hospital` types are shown below, where each hospital is assigned a quota of 2 and each applicant is assigned a default quota of 1.

```
instance Set Applicant
instance Set Hospital where quota = forall 2
```

2.3 Generating Stable Matchings

In general, a matching problem can have multiple stable matchings. However, two of them are especially significant. For our problem, these are the *hospital-optimal stable match* and the *applicant-optimal stable match*. (Sometimes the adjective "stable" is omitted for brevity.) In a hospital-optimal match, hospitals do as well as they possibly can. While not intended, the structure of the matching problem entails that a stable match where hospitals perform their best is also a stable match where applicants perform their worst [17, Chapter 2, Corollary 2.14]. Similarly, in an applicant-optimal match, applicants perform their best and hospitals their worst. Interestingly, the NRMP program was shown to be hospital optimal [21] before it was changed to be applicant optimal in 1997 [15].

A stable match can be computed with the function `twoWayWithPref`, which takes two preference encodings of the `Info` type and yields a value of type `Match a b` that stores all the elements of set `b` matched to an element of set `a`. The overloaded value `twoWay` triggers the computation by inferring the `Info` arguments from its type annotation. For example, the annotation `Match Applicant Hospital` generates the applicant-optimal matching.

```
> twoWay :: Match Applicant Hospital
{Sunny --> [], Darrius --> [City], Latha --> [General], Joseph --> [General], Arthur --> [City]}
```

Similarly, `Match Hospital Applicant` generates a hospital-optimal matching.

```
> twoWay :: Match Hospital Applicant
{City --> [Arthur,Darrius], Mercy --> [], General --> [Latha,Joseph]}
```

We can observe that the two matchings are the same. However, this need not always be the case. The DSL also provides a function `twoWayWithCapacity` to find the remaining quotas in a matching. The next example shows that General and City have exhausted their quotas of applicants, whereas Mercy's quota of 2 is untouched, since no residents have been assigned to it.

```
> twoWayWithCapacity :: Match Hospital Applicant
{City --> [Arthur,Darrius] : 0, Mercy --> [] : 2, General --> [Latha,Joseph] : 0}
```

2.4   The Role of Type Classes in the DSL Design

After examining a problem encoding in our DSL, we can now discuss an important aspect of the DSL's design: the use of type classes. In our opinion, the type classes enhance the clarity of the encoding that is generated as well as guide users during the encoding process. Using the `twoWayWithPref` function, which is the function for matching we would use in the absence of a type class, would require users to encode hospitals' and applicants' preferences without guidance from the DSL, making it more challenging. Our DSL explicitly sets user expectations, as shown below, with the first instance gathering hospitals' choices for applicants using ranks, and the second doing the reverse.

```
instance Hospital Applicant Rank where
    gather = ....

instance Applicant Hospital where
    gather = ....
```

Moreover, the declaration `twoWay :: Match Applicant Hospital` provides an easy way for users to specify that they want an applicant-optimal match. In contrast, without the type class users must call the `twoWayWithPref` function with the arguments `infoApplicant` and `infoHospital` and consider input order, which can yield different results. Finally, as we will see later, original preference encodings (`Info` values) can evolve over time. Having the initial preference list determined by an instance declaration (of the class `Preference`) improves clarity; otherwise, users would need to rely on naming conventions to identify starting preference lists.

3   Representational Ranking

The encoding of the NRMP example in the previous section is not ideal, particularly when the number of applicants or hospitals to be ranked becomes large. Instead of ranking through ordered lists, it's often more practical to use a function that computes ranks based on attributes of the elements being ranked. For example, a hospital might prefer to rank candidates using weighted criteria, such as MCAT scores, interview performance, prior experiences, and whether their previous degree is from their hospital. Each candidate's score can be generated using a formula, and the reciprocal of this score can be used to determine their rank. Different hospitals may assign various weights to these criteria, with some even omitting certain factors. MATCHMAKER facilitates this form of ranking. To this end, we define a data type `AInfo` for storing the relevant applicant data.

```
data AInfo = Appl {examScore       :: Double,
                   experience      :: Double,
                   interviewScore  :: Double,
                   sameSchool      :: Bool }
```

Similarly, a candidate might prefer to specify the ranking of hospitals implicitly based on the livability of the city the hospital is in, reputation of the programs and their personal desire to attend a particular program. Again, these criteria are assigned appropriate weights. The applicants' model of hospital preferences is captured by the data type `HInfo`, defined as follows.

```
data HInfo = Hptl {hospitalRank      :: Rank,
                   cityLivability    :: Int,
                   desirabilityScore :: Double}
```

Next we need to express the information in a form that supports the computation of preference lists.

3.1   Normalization and Weighting of Criteria

To generate rankings, we normalize values of a representation type to numbers using the type class `Norm`. Figure 3 shows the definition of this type class as well as some of its instances. The primary purpose of this type class is to transform an element of type `a` into a number between 0 and 1. For straightforward types like `Rank` and `Bool`, we can create a direct instance of this type class. Note that the `Norm` instance for the `Rank` type, which represents relative preferences, conveys that a numerically lower rank corresponds to a higher preference, and vice versa.

In most cases, a constant is required for normalization. For instance, to normalize an exam score of 80, we need to know the maximum possible score. Assuming this to be 100, the score can be normalized as $\frac{80}{100} = 0.8$. To handle this, we introduce a new data type `BoundedVal` for managing normalization with a bound. The `outOf` function is utilized to create a `BoundedVal` value for normalization. We represent this normalization as 80 `outOf` 100.[4]

Occasionally, an attribute may have negative valency, indicating that a lower value of the attribute is considered more favorable than a higher value. In Fig. 3 we define a type class `Valence` along with a data type `Polarity`. Using this type class, we can specify the desired valency of a type. For negative valence double values, we define a data type `NDouble` and its corresponding normalization. Note

---

[4] Thanks to one of the reviewers for recommending the use of the `BoundedVal` data type, which enables our `norm` function to be total.

```
class Norm a where                      data BoundedVal a = a `OutOf` Double
    components :: a -> [Double]
    components _ = []                    outOf :: (Norm a,Num a,Valence a) =>
                                                   a -> Double -> Double
    norm :: a -> Double                 outOf x y = norm (x `OutOf` y)
    norm = sum . components
                                        instance Valence NDouble where
instance Norm Bool where                    valence (ND _) = Neg
  norm x = if x then 1.0 else 0.0
                                        instance (Valence a, Num a,Norm a) =>
instance Norm Rank where                        Norm (BoundedVal a) where
    norm (Rank r) = 1/fromIntegral r        components (x `OutOf` y)
                                              | valence x == Pos = [norm x/y]
instance Norm Double where                    | otherwise        = [y/norm x]
    norm v = v
                                        class Weights a where
instance Norm Int where                     weights :: a -> [Double]
    norm v = fromIntegral v                 weights _ = [1.0]

                                        class Weights a =>
data Polarity = Pos | Neg                   Preference a b c | a b -> c where
                                            gather :: Info a b c
class Valence a where
    valence :: a -> Polarity
    valence _ = Pos

instance Valence Int
instance Valence Double
...
```

Fig. 3. Support for Representational Rankings in MATCHMAKER.

that the positions of the numerator and denominator are switched compared to the Norm instance of the Double type.

The type class Norm also offers a components function, which provides a list of normalized values corresponding to the various arguments of a constructor of an abstract data type. As shown in the class definition, once we have defined components for a data type, the normalized values can be easily deduced from it.

With the help of norm and outOf, we can define the normalization for the applicant and hospital preference representations as follows.

```
instance Norm AInfo where
    components (Appl e x i c) = [e `outOf` 800, x `outOf` 10, i `outOf` 10, norm c]

instance Norm HInfo where
    components (Hptl h c d) = [norm h, c `outOf` 10, d `outOf` 5]
```

However, before we compute preferences using the normalization of representation types, we need to address the situation where applicants or hospitals may weight criteria differently. To that end, MATCHMAKER provides a class Weights, shown in Fig. 3, which can be used to assign different weight profiles for various criteria corresponding to different constructors of type a. This type class is then placed as a class constraint in the definition of the Preference type class (shown in Fig. 2), which specifies that the first type argument of the Preference class should also be a member of the Weights class. This allows us to generate rankings for various hospitals and applicants using different distributions of criteria weights.

The weight distributions of the criteria for various hospitals and applicants are specified as instances of the Weight class. We observe that Mercy assigns

```
instance Functor (Rec b) where
  fmap f (Rec m) = Rec (fmap f m)

instance Functor (Info a b) where
  fmap f (Info m) = Info (fmap (fmap f) m)

zapRec :: Rec a (b -> c) -> Rec a b -> Rec a c
zapRec (Rec fMap) (Rec xMap) = Rec (M.intersectionWith ($) fMap xMap)

zapInfo :: (Ord a,Ord b) => Info a b (c -> d) -> Info a b c -> Info a b d
zapInfo (Info i1) (Info i2) = Info (M.intersectionWith zapRec i1 i2)

zipInfo  :: (Ord2 a b) => Info a b c -> Info a b d -> Info a b (c,d)
zipInfo i1 = zapInfo (fmap (,) i1)

zipInfo2 :: (Ord2 a b) => Info a b c -> Info a b d -> Info a b e -> Info a b (c,d,e)
zipInfo2 i1 i2 i3 = zapInfo (fmap (\x (y,z) -> (x,y,z)) i1) (zipInfo i2 i3)


completedWith  :: Ord a => (b -> c -> d) -> Info a b c -> Info a b d
completedWith2 :: Ord a => (b -> c -> d -> e) -> Info a b (c,d) -> Info a b e
```

Fig. 4. Combinators for combining `Info` values and generating them from profiles.

greater importance to exam and interview scores than to previous work experiences compared to other hospitals. Furthermore, unlike other hospitals, Mercy gives some weight to whether or not applicants have previously studied there.

```
instance Weights Hospital where
  weights Mercy = [0.3,0.3,0.3,0.1]
  weights _     = [0.2,0.2,0.6,0.0]
```

For applicants we assume that they all use the same weights for the various criteria.

```
instance Weights Applicant where
  weights = forall [0.2,0.2,0.6]
```

3.2   Representational Rankings in Action

Now we can derive a rank from preference representations. Specifically, we can replace the third argument of the `Preference` type class, `Rank`, with `AInfo` and `HInfo`, allowing us to record the preferences for hospitals and applicants, respectively. Before we look at the actual preference encodings of applicants, note that values of some criteria remain unchanged for different applicants. For example, rankings of the hospitals and the livability of the cities they are located in are not applicant dependent but intrinsic to the hospitals and cities themselves. We can exploit this fact to factor out this shared information, which can then be used by all applicants. The function `hProfile` constructs a hospital/city profile for each hospital as a partial `HInfo` value with fixed ranking and livability score information but still unassigned desirability scores of type `DScore` (which is a type synonym for `Double`).

```
hProfile :: Hospital -> DScore -> HInfo
hProfile Mercy   = Hptl (Rank 2) 9
hProfile City    = Hptl (Rank 1) 10
hProfile General = Hptl (Rank 3) 8
```

Next, we represent the desirability scores of hospitals for the different applicants in the form of an `Info` value. Of course, it may be the case that applicants use different sources for getting the ranking and livability information, resulting in non-uniform rankings of hospitals and livability scores of cities. In such a case, we could have two additional `Info` values, one each for rank and livability, similar to what we have for the desirability scores. However, for our current example we consider them to be uniform.

```
desirability :: Info Applicant Hospital DScore
desirability =
info [Arthur   --> [City --> 3],
     Sunny    --> [Mercy --> 4,City --> 3],
     Joseph   --> [Mercy --> 1,City --> 5,General --> 4],
     Latha    --> [Mercy --> 5,City --> 1,General --> 1],
     Darrius  --> [Mercy --> 5,City --> 5,General --> 4]]
```

We can combine the fixed and variable criteria values to generate the overall representation of applicants' preferences using the `completedWith` combinator. As the type of `completedWith` (shown in Fig. 4) indicates, it takes a function with output type `d` and an `Info` value with type `c` as its third type argument representing the value type of the variable criterion. It returns as output a completed `Info` value for matching set `a` with respect to `b` using the type `d`.

```
instance Preference Applicant Hospital HInfo where
  gather = hProfile `completedWith` desirability
```

We can represent the preferences for hospitals in a similar way. Again, we begin by defining the profile of applicants `aProfile` for the fixed information, which includes the applicants' exam scores and their work experience.

```
aProfile :: Applicant -> IScore -> SStatus -> AInfo
aProfile a = case a of
                Arthur  -> Appl 700 2
                Sunny   -> Appl 720 2
                Joseph  -> Appl 750 1
                Latha   -> Appl 650 5
                Darrius -> Appl 790 2
```

This leaves applicants' hospital-dependent attributes, such as interview scores `IScore` and prior student status `SStatus` at a hospital, to be filled in by the individual hospitals. The interview scores of applicants at various hospitals are recorded again in a corresponding `Info` value.

```
interview :: Info Hospital Applicant IScore
interview = info
    [Mercy    --> [Joseph --> 8,Darrius --> 9],
     City     --> [Arthur -->10,Sunny --> 9,Joseph --> 4,Latha --> 6,Darrius--> 10],
     General  --> [Arthur --> 9,Joseph --> 8,Latha --> 5,Darrius --> 10]]
```

Similarly, the student status of applicants at a given hospital is also represented by an `Info` value.

```
school :: Info Hospital Applicant SStatus
school = info
    [Mercy    -->[Joseph --> False,Darrius --> True],
     City     -->[Arthur --> True,Sunny --> False,Joseph --> False,Latha --> False,
                  Darrius --> False],
     General  -->[Arthur --> False,Joseph --> True,Latha --> False,Darrius --> False]]
```

Finally, we can combine the applicants' profiles with their interview scores and student status information to generate an `Info` value with complete information about students. We do this by first "zipping" together `interview` and `school` using the `zipInfo` function, which results in an `Info` value where the interview score and school status information for every candidate is paired up. The function `zipInfo` is analogous to Haskell's `zip` function in that it has the effect of pairing `Info` values. We also provide functions `zipInfo2`, `zipInfo3`, and so on, for combining multiple `Info` values, corresponding to Haskell's `zip2` and `zip3`. The function `completedWith2` is a function which takes as input a profile with two unassigned fields and an `Info` value that contains these variable values and produces a completed `Info` value. We provide different variants of the `compeletedWith` function to join multiple `Info` values.

```
instance Preference Hospital Applicant AInfo where
  gather = aProfile `completedWith2` (interview `zipInfo` school)
```

This completes the specification of applicant and hospital preferences. It is instructive to see that we can get concrete rankings from our preference representations. We can do so using the `ranks` function (defined in Fig. 2) as shown below. Note that the preference lists of hospitals are unchanged from Fig. 1. Similarly, we can verify that the preference lists for applicants have not changed either.

```
> ranks (gather :: Info Hospital Applicant AInfo)
{City    --> [Darrius,Arthur,Sunny,Latha,Joseph] : 2,
 Mercy   --> [Darrius,Joseph] : 2,
 General --> [Darrius,Arthur,Joseph,Latha] : 2}
```

The stable matchings can be generated in the same way as we did with explicit rankings.

```
> twoWay :: Match Hospital Applicant
{City --> [Arthur,Darrius], Mercy --> [], General --> [Latha,Joseph]}
```

Since the inferred preference lists for applicants and hospitals didn't change, the stable matchings don't change either.

4   Evolution and Analysis of Matches

So far we have seen matching problems with a fixed initial set of agents. Let's assume now that some hospitals or applicants decide to amend their preferences or maybe some hospitals or applicants are added late in the NRMP cycle and need to be accommodated in the match. The straightforward thing to do would be to manually modify the preference lists and rerun the matching algorithm on this amended list. Not only is this approach prone to errors during the update, but we would also lose track of the history of the different stages of the process, which can reveal how changes in the data lead to changes in matches. An alternative is to keep the original and amend it using functions provided by the DSL. This approach makes the changes explicit, allowing users to track the evolution of data and corresponding matchings. The type signatures for some of the relevant functions for these tasks are shown in Fig. 5.

```
modWithRanks :: Ord2 a b => Info a b Rank -> (a,[b]) -> Info a b Rank
modWithInfo  :: Ord2 a b => Info a b c -> Info a b c -> Info a b c
modWithRow   :: Ord2 a b => Info a b c -> (a,[(b,c)]) -> Info a b c

updateWithRow   :: Ord2 a b => Info a b c -> (a,[(b,c)]) -> Info a b c
updateWithInfo  :: Ord2 a b => Info a b c -> Info a b c -> Info a b c
updateWithInfos :: Ord2 a b => Info a b c -> [Info a b c] -> Info a b c

modWithRanksDef :: (Ord2 a b,Preference a b Rank) => (a,[b]) -> Info a b Rank
...

data CompMatch a b = CompMatch {unCompMatch :: [(a,[b],[b])]}

diffMatch  :: Eq2 a b => Match a b -> Match a b -> CompMatch a b
twoWayDiff :: Info a b c -> Info a b c -> CompMatch a b
```

Fig. 5. Combinators to modify encodings and compare results.

4.1   Updating Ranks and Adding Agents

Assume that a new applicant Bob is added to the matching process. Like other
applicants, Bob will have his preference list of hospitals. Hospitals will also need
to accommodate him in their preference lists. Let's further assume that City
decides not to rank him. Situations like this are of special interests to game
theorists who are interested in finding out how the addition of a new applicant
or a hospital might change the resulting match. For example, is it more favorable
to the applicants or the hospitals? In this section, we look at how MATCHMAKER
can be used to support such investigations.

We begin by updating the `Applicant` data type to include the `Bob` constructor.

```
data Applicant = Arthur | Sunny | Joseph | Latha | Darrius | Bob
```

We can update the preference list of applicants by adding Bob's preferences
using the `modWithRanks` function. It takes as input the original preference list of
applicants as well as the new applicant to be added with his preference list. The
function `gather` provides the original encoding of the preferences for applicants.

```
updatedAppl = gather `modWithRanks` (Bob --> [Mercy, City, General])
```

We also update the preference lists for hospitals. Note how we can chain
together multiple updates. A difference between the two values `updatedAppl` and
`updatedHosp` is that, while the former creates a new record for Bob, the latter
simply updates the already existing preference lists for Mercy and General.

```
updatedHosp = gather `modWithRanks` (Mercy   --> [Darrius,Bob,Joseph])
                     `modWithRanks` (General --> [Bob,Darrius,Arthur,Joseph,Latha])
```

When we need to modify the preference lists of multiple agents, rather than
making one change at a time by chaining together multiple `modWithRanks` calls,
it is more convenient to collect all the changes in an `Info` value and update
the original encoding with it in one go. This can be done with the `modWithInfo`
function, as shown below. The updated preferences of Mercy and General are
stored in an `Info` value called `deltaInfo`, which can then be used to update

the original preference encoding of the applicants. Note that since City doesn't appear in `deltaInfo`, its preferences are not changed in `updatedHosp`.

```
deltaInfo = choices [Mercy    --> [Darrius,Bob,Joseph],
                     General  --> [Bob,Darrius,Arthur,Joseph,Latha]]

updatedHosp = gather `modWithInfo` deltaInfo
```

The function `modWithInfo` is useful for various reasons. When the number of elements being matched is large, we can keep the original data and the intended changes separate. If we need to make iterative changes, this approach keeps track of the changes performed in each iteration. We can also contemplate alternative changes to the data. We also have a `modWithInfos` combinator, which can be used to modify the original data with a list of iterative changes stored as `Info` values themselves. For example, the following expression modifies the data by four updates `i1, ..., i4`.

```
updated = gather `modWithInfos` [i1,i2,i3,i4]
```

If at any point we need to undo some of the changes, we can simply remove the corresponding `Info` value from the list.

Now that we have the amended preference lists for hospitals and applicants, we can use them to get new matchings using the `twoWayWithPref` function, which was introduced in Sect. 2.2.

```
> twoWayWithPref updatedHosp updatedAppl
{City --> [Arthur,Darrius], General --> [Latha,Joseph], Mercy --> [Bob]}
```

Notice how the matching is different from the original matchings, repeated here for convenience.

```
> twoWay :: Match Hospital Applicant
{City --> [Arthur,Darrius], General --> [Latha,Joseph], Mercy --> []}
```

Clearly, Mercy has benefited by gaining a resident. While figuring out the difference was trivial in our current example, spotting changes in even a moderately large example is more difficult. To do so systematically, we provide a function called `diffMatch`, which compares two `Match` values and reports the difference between the two matchings. In our current example, we obtain the following.

```
> diffMatch twoWay (twoWayWithPref updatedHosp updatedAppl)
{Mercy --> [] => [Bob]}
```

The result `Mercy --> [] => [Bob]` shows that that Mercy went from not having any resident in the original match to having Bob in the updated match. An interesting thing to note here is that even though we didn't annotate the type of the first argument `twoWay`, it can be inferred from the type of the second argument of `diffMatch`.

What can we say about the performance of various hospitals and applicants in the updated match, compared to the original match? Intuitively, it seems that most hospitals, namely City and General, have performed as well as they did before, while Mercy has improved its performance. Similarly, it appears that no applicants have performed worse than in the original match. Do these observations always hold? Game theory informs us that no hospital will be worse off, and some hospitals are better off compared to the original match [17, Theorem 2.26]. At the same time, none of the original applicants are better off, while some can be worse off than in the original match. In any case, MATCHMAKER can be employed as a tool for gaining a deeper understanding of a wide range of matching scenarios.

4.2   Updating Representational Ranks

Assume that we want to update the representational ranks of our example from Sect. 3.2. More concretely, suppose Mercy wants to add Sunny and Arthur, and City wants to add Sunny to their preference lists. They only need to provide the interview scores and school status for the applicants, as the other information can be obtained from the applicants' profiles. The interview scores can be updated for the two hospitals using the `updateWithRow` combinator, which takes an `Info` value to be updated along with the information to update it with. An entry such as `City --> [Sunny --> 9]` indicates that City assigns an interview score of 9 to Sunny, which is then appended to its already existing score assignments for other applicants. The function `updateWithRow` can be chained together to update the records for multiple hospitals.

```
interview1 = interview `updateWithRow` (City  --> [Sunny --> 9])
                       `updateWithRow` (Mercy --> [Sunny --> 8,Arthur --> 8])
```

And the school status also needs to be updated.

```
school1 = school `updateWithRow` (Mercy --> [Sunny --> True,Arthur --> False])
                 `updateWithRow` (City  --> [Sunny --> False])
```

Again, we also have the option to collect all changes in an `Info` value, which is then used by the `updateWithInfo` combinator.

```
deltaInterview = info [Mercy --> [Sunny --> 8,Arthur --> 8],City --> [Sunny --> 9]]

interview1 = interview `updateWithInfo` deltaInterview
```

Finally, we can use the modified interview scores and school status information to update the preferences for hospitals.

```
updatedHosp = aProfile `completedWith2` (interview1 `zipInfo` school1)
```

The changed data leads to the following preference lists for various hospitals.

```
> ranks updatedHosp
{Mercy   --> [Darrius,Sunny,Arthur,Joseph] : 2,
 City    --> [Darrius,Arthur,Sunny,Latha,Joseph] : 2,
 General --> [Darrius,Arthur,Joseph,Latha] : 2}
```

We can now generate the updated match using the `twoWayWithPref` function. But perhaps it will be more interesting to see how this matching differs from the original match. As shown, the only difference in the two matchings is that Mercy which was not assigned a resident initially, now has Sunny assigned to it.

```
> twoWayDiff updatedHosp gather
{Mercy --> [] => [Sunny]}
```

```
class Preference a b c => Exchange a b where
  endowment :: Match a b

type SameSetMatch a = Maybe (Match a a)

data CompRanks a b = CompRanks {unCompRanks :: [(a,[(b,Rank)],[(b,Rank)])]}

oneWay :: (Preference a b c,Set2 a b,Norm c) => Match a b

oneWayWithOrder :: (Preference a b c,Set2 a b,Norm c) => [a] -> Match a b
oneWayWithPref  :: (Preference a b c, Set2 a b,Norm c) => Info a b c -> Match a b

trade   :: (Preference a b c,Set2 a b,Norm c) => Match a b
sameSet :: (Preference a a b,Set a,Norm b) => SameSetMatch a

diffRanks :: (Eq2 a b,Preference a b c,Set2 a b,Norm c) => Match a b -> Match a b ->
             CompRanks a b
```

Fig. 6. Some type and function definitions for various matching problems.

5 Other Matching Problems

In addition to the two-way stable matching problem, MATCHMAKER also allows for the modeling of other interesting matching problems like one-sided matchings, one-sided matching with exchange, and same-set matchings, which we briefly discuss in this section. The various types and function definitions used in this section are shown in Fig. 6.

5.1 Bipartite Matching with One-Sided Preferences

The first important example of a one-sided matching problem is known as the *house allocation problem* in the economics literature. In this type of matching, only the elements in the source set have preferences for the elements in the target set. The preferences of the target sets are not taken into account. Some of its applications have been allocating graduates to trainee positions, students to projects, professors to offices, and clients to servers.

As a concrete example, let us consider the problem of selecting kidney donors for various transplant patients. Assume that the donors are altruistic and don't care who their kidney goes to. Patients, on the other hand, have a preference over the kidneys: a good kidney for a patient depends on the tissue compatibility of the donor-recipient pair as well as the donor's age and their overall health condition. Thus, the transplant team of a patient may have a ranked preference list of donors. Figure 7a shows patients with their preference lists.

Formally, the donor assignment problem is a three-tuple (T, D, P), where $T = \{t_1, \ldots, t_k\}$ is a finite set of transplant patients and $D = \{d_1, \ldots, d_n\}$ is a finite set of donors. P is a preference map such that the preference of each patient $t \in T$ is represented by an ordered list of preferences $P(t)$ on set D. We assume that each patient has a quota of 1, that is, they can be assigned just one donor. A matching $\mu : T \to D$ in this case is a partial function that assigns every patient to 1 donor.

We can represent the patient-donor example with the machinery already developed for two-sided matching. Figure 7 shows an encoding of the problem

P_1	P_2	P_3	P_4
Bob	Alice	Alice	Alice
Dan	Dan	Bob	Bob
Dillon	Dillon	Dillon	Dan

(a) Preference lists of Donors
to Patients.

```
data Donor = Alice | Bob | Dan | Dillon
data Patient = P1 | P2 | P3 | P4

instance Preference Patient Donor Rank where
gather = choices [P1 --> [Bob,Dan,Dillon],
                  P2 --> [Alice,Dan,Dillon],
                  P3 --> [Alice,Bob,Dillon],
                  P4 --> [Alice,Bob,Dan]]
```

(b) Encoding the example in DSL.

Fig. 7. Assigning donors to patients: Bipartite matching with one-sided preferences.

using explicit ranks. In a more realistic setting, the agency tasked with performing the match might prefer to rank the donors using meaningful representation such as age and the blood and tissue compatibility between the donor-patient pair.

How do we assign donors to the patients based on their preferences? The strategy we use here is the so-called *serial dictatorship mechanism* [1]. It is a straightforward greedy algorithm that takes each patient in turn and assigns them to the most preferred available donor on their preference list. The order in which the patients are processed will, in general, affect the outcome. In applications where elements have a quota of n, they are assigned to n objects when their turn comes for processing. For our example here, we expect that a matching agency will come up with an order of processing based on factors such as the urgency of a patient's situation, their age, or their time on the waiting list. The function `oneWayWithOrder` performs serial dictatorship with a given order as shown below where patient P_3 gets its first choice donor, P_4 gets its first choice amongst the remaining donors, and so on.

```
> oneWayWithOrder [P3,P4,P2,P1] :: Match Patient Donor
{P1 --> [Dillon],P2 --> [Dan],P3 --> [Alice],P4 --> [Bob]}
```

Oftentimes users might prefer that the matching function infer a preferred order based on position of the constructor in the data definition for donors, that is, the `Donor` data definition implies an order of `[P1,P2,P3,P4]`. The function `oneWay` generates a one-way match with this implicit order.

```
> oneWay :: Match Patient Donor
{P1 --> [Bob],P2 --> [Alice],P3 --> [Dillon],P4 --> [Dan]}
```

Finally, there is also a third variant of the function `oneWayWithPref` that takes explicit preference encoding like its counterpart `twoWayWithPref`.

As we can see, these two matches are different because they are generated using different orders. Is one better than the other? What is the best possible match among the various possibilities? Manually comparing one match with another is cumbersome because for every patient we have to look at the two matchings and compare the relative ranks of the two donors in that patient's preference list. This task is simplified by the function `diffRanks`, which compares the ranks of the two matchings using a type called `CompRanks`. This type represents for every agent the element assigned to them in those matchings as

well the elements' ranks for comparison. In the following expression, we use
x = oneWayWithOrder [P3,P4,P2,P1].

```
> diffRanks oneWay x :: CompRanks Patient Donor
{P1 --> Bob : 1 > Dillon : 3, P2 --> Alice : 1 > Dan : 2,
 P3 --> Dillon : 3 < Alice : 1, P4 --> Dan : 3 < Bob : 2}
```

The first match is advantageous for patients P_1 and P_2, whereas the second
match is advantageous for patients P_3 and P_4. Informally, a matching is *Pareto
optimal* if there is no other matching in which some patient is better off, whilst
no patient is worse off. It is used as a metric to compare the quality of outcomes
in game theoretic matchings. The deceptively simple-looking *serial dictatorship*
algorithm results in Pareto optimal matchings, which implies that for any two
matchings, there are some patients for whom one match is better and for some,
the second match is better. In other words, a unique best match doesn't exist.

5.2   Bipartite Matching with One-Sided Preferences and Exchange

We assumed the presence of altruistic donors in our last example. However, kidneys are valuable commodities, and altruistic donors alone can't fulfill the vast
demand for them. A more realistic scenario is a family member or a friend donat-
ing one of their kidneys to a loved one. However, sometimes this donation may
not happen due to reasons like tissue or blood group incompatibility. An elegant
solution was developed in the field of economics. Suppose (d_1, r_1) and (d_2, r_2) are
two donor-receiver pairs such that d_i wants to donate to r_i but can't do so. However, if d_1 could donate to r_2 and d_2 to r_1, then both the patients would be able
to receive kidneys. This could be easily scaled to multiple pairs generating large
numbers of compatibility pairs. The actual *kidney exchange mechanism* [16] is a
little more complicated, but the exchange between multiple donor-receiver pairs
is at the heart of it. This exchange characterizes our next matching algorithm,
the so-called *top trading cycle* (TTC) matching mechanism for one-way matching where every element has an initial endowment and a preference list [18]. The
resulting match takes both of these into account.

Take the patient-donor example we considered in the last section. At the
start, some donor, presumably family or friends willing to donate a kidney, is
assigned to each patient. These initial set of donors are sometimes also called
the *initial endowment*, or just *endowment*, of a patient. Assume that patients
$P_1, \ldots, P_4$ are endowed with Bob, Dan, Alice, and Dillon, respectively, such
that all the patients are compatible with the donors they are endowed with. In
this case, TTC tries to find out if the patients can do better than the donor
they are assigned to, based on their preference lists. We start by representing
endowments for which we define the multi-parameter type class Exchange, which
has a Preference class constraint (see Fig. 6). The instance definition of Exchange
for our example is as follows.

```
instance Exchange Patient Donor where
    endowment = assign [P1 --> Bob,P2 --> Dillon,P3 --> Alice,P4 --> Dan]
```

Now we can use the function trade provided by the DSL to generate the matching.

```
> trade :: Match Patient Donor
{P1 --> [Bob], P2 --> [Dan], P3 --> [Alice], P4 --> [Dillon]}
```

Did any patient gain as a result of the change? We can use the diffRanks function
we saw in the previous section to find out. We discover that patients P_2 and P_4
do indeed profit by exchanging their donors.

```
> diffRanks endowment trade :: CompRanks Patient Donor
{P2 --> Dillon : 3 < Dan : 2, P4 --> Dan : 3 < Dillon : 2}
```

5.3 Same-Set Matching

This variation of the problem is the so-called *stable roommate problem* [6,9]
where the source and the target sets being matched are the same. For example,
a set of students living in the dormitory can supply a ranked preference list of
other students they want to be roommates with. An example is shown below.

```
data Student = Charlie | Peter | Kelly | Sam

instance Preference Student Student Rank where
    gather = choices [Charlie --> [Peter,Sam,Kelly],  Peter --> [Kelly,Sam,Charlie],
                      Kelly   --> [Peter,Charlie,Sam], Sam   --> [Charlie,Kelly,Peter]]
```

We can obtain a stable matching of roommates using Irving's algorithm [8]. In
order to capture the fact that the source and target sets are the same, we define a
type synonym SameSetMatch that assigns the same type a to both the source and
the target sets in the Match type (see Fig. 6). Even though same-set matchings are
stable matching problems like the bipartite two-sided matching problems, they
are different in that a stable match always exists for the former, whereas it may
not always exist for the latter. This fact is reflected by the Maybe constructor
in the type definition of SameSetMatch. Finally, we can generate the same-set
matching using the sameSet function, which produces the following result for our
example from above.

```
> sameSet :: SameSetMatch Student
Just {Charlie --> [Sam], Peter --> [Kelly]}
```

6 Related Work

Matching [20] is a library for Python that allows users to encode simple matching
problems in a straightforward manner. An issue with the library is that all the
encoding are done using strings, which makes error handling difficult and thus
complicates the maintenance and debugging of larger examples. In comparison,
MATCHMAKER avails the strongly typed feature of the host language Haskell to
detect the various errors in encoding.

Similarly, *matchingMarkets* [10] is a matching library for R. The advantage
of the library is that it implements a wide variety of matching algorithms developed in the matching theory. Additionally, it implements statistical tools to
correct for the sample selection bias from observed outcomes in matching markets, which is something that MATCHMAKER doesn't do. The library encodes

the preference relation between the sets of elements being matched in the form of a matrix. While an efficient way to encode the preferences, the matrix encoding is clunky and is thus difficult to understand, update and maintain. Another stable matching library for R and C++ *matchingR* is [19], which uses matrices to encode the preference relations and thus suffers from the same problems as *matchingMarkets*.

MATCHMAKER allows users to specify their preferences more abstractly in terms of attributes that they understand, while all the previous libraries only allow specification of preference in terms of ranks. Additionally, none of these libraries offers either the primitives for systematic modification of representations or primitives to compare and contrast different matchings.

Matching problems can also be solved using constraint programming [5,13] or SMT solving [3]. Moreover, integer linear programming can be used to solve NP-hard stable marriage problems, including ones with ties and incomplete lists as well as the many-to-one generalization [2]. While powerful, a potential downside is that encoding matching problems as constraints might be challenging for users. In contrast, MATCHMAKER facilitates high-level representations of matching problems and can thus be used without any specialized knowledge.

7   Conclusions

MATCHMAKER is an embedded DSL in Haskell for expressing, solving, and analyzing game-theoretic matching problems. Our implementation leverages advanced type system features of Haskell to facilitate high-level representations of matching problems, expressed in terms of domain elements. MATCHMAKER also supports the maintenance and evolution of the problem representation and provides some limited support for analyzing computed results, making it a useful tool for end users as well as game theorists.

The design of our DSL emphasizes the significance of strong typing in detecting errors at compile time. Additionally, employing multi-parameter type classes promotes a lucid mental representation of the problem, helping users to comprehend problem structures and implement complex functions.

References

1. Bogomolnaia, A., Moulin, H.: A new solution to the random assignment problem. J. Econ. Theory **100**(2), 295–328 (2001)
2. Delorme, M., García, S., Gondzio, J., Kalcsics, J., Manlove, D., Pettersson, D.: Mathematical models for stable matching problems with ties and incomplete lists. Eur. J. Oper. Res. **277**(2), 426–441 (2019)
3. Drummond, J., Perrault, A., Bacchus, F.: Sat is an effective and complete method for solving stable matching problems with couples. In: Proceedings of the 24th International Conference on Artificial Intelligence, IJCAI 2015, pp. 518–525. AAAI Press (2015)
4. Gale, D., Shapley, L.S.: College admissions and the stability of marriage. Am. Math. Monthly **69**(1), 9–15 (1962)

5. Gent, I.P., Irving, R.W., Manlove, D.F., Prosser, P., Smith, B.M.: A constraint programming approach to the stable marriage problem. In: Walsh, T. (ed.) CP 2001. LNCS, vol. 2239, pp. 225–239. Springer, Heidelberg (2001). https://doi.org/10.1007/3-540-45578-7_16
6. Gusfield, D.: The structure of the stable roommate problem: efficient representation and enumeration of all stable assignments. SIAM J. Comput. **17**(4), 742–769 (1988)
7. Gusfield, D., Irving, R.W.: The Stable Marriage Problem: Structure and Algorithms. MIT Press, Cambridge (1989)
8. Irving, R.W.: An efficient algorithm for the "stable roommates" problem. J. Algor. **6**(4), 577–595 (1985)
9. Irving, R.W., Leather, P.: The complexity of counting stable marriages. SIAM J. Comput. **15**(3), 655–667 (1986)
10. Klein, T., Aue, R., Giegerich, S., Sauer, A.: matchingMarkets: Analysis of Stable Matchings in R (2020). https://matchingmarkets.org/
11. Manlove, D.F.: Algorithmics of Matching Under Preferences. World Scientific, Singapore (2013)
12. NRMP: National Resident Matching Program (2022). https://www.nrmp.org/intro-to-the-match/how-matching-algorithm-works/
13. Prosser, P.: Stable roommates and constraint programming. In: CPAIOR (2014)
14. Roth, A.E.: Deferred acceptance algorithms: History, theory, practice, and open questions. Working Paper 13225, National Bureau of Economic Research (2007)
15. Roth, A.E., Peranson, E.: The redesign of the matching market for American physicians: some engineering aspects of economic design. Am. Econ. Rev. **89**(4), 748–780 (1999)
16. Roth, A.E., Sönmez, T., Ünver, M.U.: Kidney exchange. Q. J. Econ. **119**(2), 457–488 (2004)
17. Roth, A.E., Sotomayor, M.A.O.: Two-Sided Matching: A Study in Game-Theoretic Modeling and Analysis. Econometric Society Monographs, Cambridge University Press, Cambridge (1990)
18. Shapley, L., Scarf, H.: On cores and indivisibility. J. Math. Econ. **1**(1), 23–37 (1974)
19. Tilly, J., Janetos, N.: matchingR: Matching Algorithms in R and C++ (2020). https://github.com/jtilly/matchingR/
20. Wilde, H., Knight, V., Gillard, J.: Matching: a python library for solving matching games. J. Open Source Softw. **5**(48), 2169 (2020)
21. Williams, K.J., Werth, V.P., Wolff, J.A.: An analysis of the resident match. New Engl. J. Med. **304**(19), 1165–1166 (1981)

Nearly Macro-free microKanren

Jason Hemann[1]([✉])[iD] and Daniel P. Friedman[2][iD]

[1] Seton Hall University, South Orange, USA
jason.hemann@shu.edu
[2] Indiana University, Bloomington, USA
dfried@indiana.edu

Abstract. We describe changes to the microKanren implementation that make it more practical to use in a host language without macros. With some modest runtime features common to most languages, we show how an implementer lacking macros can come closer to the expressive power that macros usually provide—with varying degrees of success. The result is a still functional microKanren that invites slightly shorter programs, and is relevant even to implementers that enjoy macro support. For those without it, we address some pragmatic concerns that necessarily occur without macros so they can better weigh their options.

CCS Concepts: • **Software and its engineering** → **Constraint and logic languages**.

Keywords: logic programming, miniKanren, DSLs, embedding, macros

ACM Reference Format:
Jason Hemann and Daniel P. Friedman. 2023. Nearly Macro-free microKanren. In *Proceedings of Symposium on Trends in Functional Programming (TFP '23)*. ACM, New York, NY, USA, 20 pages. https://doi.org/XXXXXXX.XXXXXXX

1 Introduction

Initially we designed microKanren [6] as a compact relational language kernel to undergird a miniKanren implementation. Macros implement the surrounding higher-level miniKanren operators and surface syntax. microKanren is often used as a tool for understanding the guts of a relational language through studying its implementation. By re-implementing miniKanren as separate surface syntax over a macro-less and side-effect free microKanren kernel, we hoped to simultaneously aid implementers when studying the source code, and also to make the language easier to port to other hosts that support programming with functions. To support both of those efforts, we also chose to program in a deliberately small and workaday set of Scheme primitives.

TFP '23, January 13-15, 2023, Boston, Massachusetts
© 2023 Association for Computing Machinery.
ACM ISBN 978-1-4503-XXXX-X/18/06...$15.00
https://doi.org/XXXXXXX.XXXXXXX
S. Chang (Ed.): TFP 2023, LNCS 13868, pp. 72–91, 2023.
https://doi.org/10.1007/978-3-031-38938-2_5

The sum of those implementation restrictions, however, seemed to force some awkward choices including: binary logical operators, one at a time local variable introduction, and leaks in the stream abstractions. These made the surface syntax macros seem almost required, and were far enough from our goals that *The Reasoned Schemer, 2nd Ed* [4] did not use a macro-less functional kernel. It also divided host languages into those that used macros and those that did not. We bridge some of that split by re-implementing parts of the kernel using some modest runtime features common to many languages.

Here we:

- show how to functionally implement more general logical operators, cleanly obviating some of the surface macros,
- survey the design space of macro-less, mostly side-effect free implementation alternatives for the remaining macros in the *TRS2e* core language implementation, and weigh the trade-offs and real-world consequences, and
- suggest practical solutions for completely eliminating the macros in those places where the purest microKanren implementations seemed impractical.

This resulted in some higher-level (variadic rather than just binary) operators, a more succinct kernel language, and enabled some performance improvement. Around half of the changes are applicable to any microKanren implementation, and the more concise goal combinators of Section 3 may also be of interest to implementers who embed goal-oriented languages like Icon [5]. The other half are necessarily awkward yet practical strategies for those platforms lacking macro support. The source code for both our re-implementation and our experimental results is available at https://github.com/jasonhemann/tfp-2023/.

In Section 2, we illustrate by example what seemed to force surface syntax macros. In Section 3, we implement conjunction and disjunction, and in Section 4 we discuss the re-implementation of the impure operators. We discuss the remaining macros in Section 5. We close with a discussion of the performance impacts of these implementation choices, and consider how implementers of Kanren languages in other hosts might benefit from these alternatives.

2 The Problem

We briefly reprise here some basics of programming in the miniKanren implementation of *TRS2e*. Although based on microKanren, the *TRS2e* implementation makes some concessions to efficiency and safety and uses a few macros in the language kernel itself. In addition to that implementation, in this paper we make occasional references to earlier iterations such as Hemann et al. [7], an expanded archival version of the 2013 paper [6].

2.1 Background

Programs consist of a database of relation definitions and queries executed in the context of those definitions. A relation definition consists of a name for the relation and a number of parameters equal to the relations arity, and then a body. This body states the condition under which the relationship holds between the parameters. Parameters range over a domain of terms, and the programmer can introduce local auxiliary variables as needed. The core *TRS2e* language implementation relies on macros fresh, defrel, and run to introduce new logic variables, globally define relations, and execute queries. Relations can refer to themselves or one another in their definitions; the whole database of relations is mutually-recursively defined. The programmer states the relation body as a logical expression, built up with conjunctions and disjunctions, over a class of equations and primitive constraints on terms. Take the carmelit-subway relation of Listing 1 as a concrete example. The Carmelit in Haifa is the world's shortest subway system with only six stations on its line; carmelit-subway is a six-place relation modeling a passenger riding that subway end to end. carmel-center, golomb, masada, etc. are all term constants in the program; each is the name of a stop on the line. The sub-expression (== a 'carmel-center) is an equation between the parameter a and the term carmel-center. The conde operator (the e is for "every line") takes any number of parenthesized sequences of expressions. Each parenthesized sequence represents the conjunction of those expressions, and the meaning of the conde expression represents the disjunction of those conjunctions. Altogether, this program states that there are two ways to ride the subway end to end: a passenger can either start at carmel-center and travel five stops to downtown, or start at downtown and travel five stops to carmel-center.

Each query against the database contains some expression the programmer wants to satisfy and introduces some number of variables against which the language should express the answer. Each query asks either for all, or some bounded number of answers. The run expression of Listing 1 is a query—it asks for at most three ways a passenger could have ridden the Carmelit, printed as a list of six values for variables $s_0 \ldots s_5$. miniKanren returns a list of two answers, the only two ways a passenger could ride the whole subway end to end.

2.2   Limitations of microKanren

A six station subway line is an example sufficiently small that modeling it should be painless. Without the higher-level operators that the miniKanren macros implement, however, that same relation requires 11 logical operator nodes, because microKanren only provides *binary* conjunctions and disjunctions. In our view, this makes the superficial syntax macros practically mandatory, and impedes host languages without a macro system. For a logic programming language, solely binary logical operators is too low level.

Moreover, the microKanren language doesn't offer the programmer sufficient guidance in using that fine-grained control. With n goals, the programmer can associate to the left, to the right, or some mixtures of the two. The syntax does not obviously encourage any one choice. Subtle changes in program structure can have profound effects on performance, and mistakes are easy to make.

Similarly, the soft-cut operator ifte in the *TRS2e* language kernel is also low level. It permits a single test, a single consequent, and a single alternative. To construct an if-then-else cascade, a microKanren programmer without the conda surface macro would need to code that unrolled conditional expression by hand.

```
(defrel (carmelit-subway a b c d e f)
  (conde
    ((== a 'carmel-center)
     (== b 'golomb)
     (== c 'masada)
     (== d 'haneviim)
     (== e 'hadar-city-hall)
     (== f 'downtown))
    ((== a 'downtown)
     (== b 'hadar-city-hall)
     (== c 'haneviim)
     (== d 'masada)
     (== e 'golomb)
     (== f 'carmel-center))))

> (run 3 (s₀ s₁ s₂ s₃ s₄ s₅)
    (carmelit-subway s₀ s₁ s₂ s₃ s₄ s₅))
'((carmel-center golomb masada
    haneviim hadar-city-hall downtown)
  (downtown hadar-city-hall haneviim
    masada golomb carmel-center))
```

Listing 1. The Carmelit subway relation and a query. Results reformatted for clarity and space.

In earlier renditions of related work, the strictures of pure functional shallow embedding—without macros—seemed to force implementations of variable introduction, relation definition, and the query interface that suffered from harsh downsides. We will revisit those earlier implementations and their trade-offs, survey the available options, and suggest compromises for those truly without macros, thus increasing microKanren's *practical* portability.

3 The Disjunction and Conjunction Goal Constructors

microKanren's binary disj₂ and conj₂ operators, shown in Listing 2, are goal combinators: they each take two goals, and produce a new goal. A *goal* is what the program attempts to achieve: it can fail or succeed (and it can succeed multiple times). A goal executes with respect to a *state*, here the curried parameter s, and the result is a *stream* of states, usually denoted s∞ as each entry in the stream is a state that results from achieving that goal in the given state. Disjunction and conjunction work slightly differently. The append∞ function used in disj₂ is a kernel primitive that combines two streams into one, with an interleave mechanism to prevent starvation; the result is a stream of the ways to achieve the two goals' disjunction. The append-map∞ function used in conj₂ is to append∞ what append-map is to append. The ways to achieve the conjunction of two goals are all the ways to achieve the second goal in a state

```
(define ((disj₂ g₁ g₂) s)
  (append∞ (g₁ s) (g₂ s)))

(define ((conj₂ g₁ g₂) s)
  (append-map∞ g₂ (g₁ s)))

(define-syntax disj
  (syntax-rules ()
    ((disj g) g)
    ((disj g₁ g₂ g* ...)
     (disj₂ g₁ (disj g₂ g* ...)))))

(define-syntax conj
  (syntax-rules ()
    ((conj g) g)
    ((conj g₁ g₂ g* ...)
     (conj (conj₂ g₁ g₂) g* ...))))
```

Listing 2. microKanren disj₂, conj₂, and macros that use them

that results from achieving the first goal. append-map∞ runs the second goal over the stream of results from the first goal, and combines together the results of mapping into a single stream. That stream represents the conjunction of the two goals, again with special attention to interleaving and starvation.

We want to implement disjunction and conjunction as functions taking arbitrary quantities of goals. These implementations should subsume the binary disj₂ and conj₂ and they also should not use apply. Nor should our implementations induce a tortured program and extraneous closures to *avoid* using apply; we address this somewhat-cryptic requirement in Section 3.2. This re-implementation requires a host that supports variable arity functions, a widely available feature included in such languages as JavaScript, Ruby, Java, and Python. These languages do not generally support macros, and so we advise implementers working in such languages to use the present approach.

3.1   Calculating the Solutions

A developer might derive these definitions as follows. We start with the definition of a recursive disj macro like one might define as surface syntax over the microKanren disj₂. As this is not part of the microKanren language, we would like to dispense with the macro and implement this behavior functionally. At the cost of an apply, we can build the corresponding explicitly recursive disj function. Since disj produces and consumes goals, we can η-expand that first functional definition by a curried parameter s. We then split disj into two mutually-recursive functions. We use the symbol ⊂ here to indicate that the newer disj produces the same values as the old one, although it now does so by calling a new globally-defined function D. This new help function will only ever be called from disj so does not *need* to be global; we do so for space and clarity. In this paper, every such help function we introduce with ⊂ could have instead been local and the relationship actually an equality.

```
(define (disj g . g*)
  (cond
    ((null? g*) g)
    (else (disj₂ g (apply disj g*)))))
= { η-expansion }
(define ((disj g . g*) s)
  (cond
    ((null? g*) (g s))
    (else ((disj₂ g (apply disj g*)) s))))
⊂
(define ((disj g . g*) s)
  (D g g* s))

(define (D g g* s)
  (cond
    ((null? g*) (g s))
    (else ((disj₂ g (apply disj g*)) s))))
```

In that version of D, we can replace the call to disj₂ by its definition in terms of append∞ and perform a trivial β-reduction. The explicit s argument suggests removing the call to apply and making D self-recursive. The definition of disj remains unchanged from before.

```
= { by definition of disj₂ }
(define (D g g* s)
  (cond
    ((null? g*) (g s))
    (else
      ((λ (s)
         (append∞ (g s) ((apply disj g*) s)))
       s))))
= { β-reduction }
(define (D g g* s)
  (cond
    ((null? g*) (g s))
    (else
      (append∞ (g s) ((apply disj g*) s)))))
= { by definition of disj }
(define (D g g* s)
  (cond
    ((null? g*) (g s))
    (else
      (append∞ (g s) (D (car g*) (cdr g*) s)))))
```

```
(define ((disj . g*) s)
  (cond
    ((null? g*) '())
    (else (D ((car g*) s) (cdr g*) s))))

(define (D s∞ g* s)
  (cond
    ((null? g*) s∞)
    (else
     (append∞ s∞
       (D ((car g*) s) (cdr g*) s)))))

(define ((conj . g*) s)
  (cond
    ((null? g*) (cons s '()))
    (else (C (cdr g*) ((car g*) s)))))

(define (C g* s∞)
  (cond
    ((null? g*) s∞)
    (else
     (C (cdr g*)
       (append-map∞ (car g*) s∞)))))
```

Listing 3. Final re-definitions of `disj` and `conj`

In both clauses of D we combine g and s, this suggests constructing that stream in `disj` and passing it along. Adding the trivial base case to that `disj` yields the definition in Listing 3.

In the appendix, we derive the definition of `conj` from Listing 3 via a similar process.

Both of these new versions are shallow wrappers over simple folds. The first steps are to dispense with the trivial case, and then to call a recursive help function that makes no use of variadic arguments. The focus is on recurring over the list g*. Unlike D, the function C does not take in the state s; the help function does not need the state for conjunction.

3.2   What's Left?

More importantly, while both the functional and the macro based versions of `disj` use a right fold, the implementation of conjunctions in Listing 3 uses a left fold over the goals. This left-fold implementation of conjunctions therefore left-associates the conjuncts. This is not an accident.

Folklore suggests left associating conjunctions tends to improve performance of miniKanren's interleaving search. The authors know of no thorough algorithmic proof of such claims, but see for instance discussions and implementation in Rosenblatt et al. [10] for some of the related work so far. We have generally, however, resorted to small step visualizations of the search tree to explain the performance impact. It is worth considering if we can make an equally compelling argument for this preference through equational reasoning and comparing the implementations of functions.

Compare the preceding derivation from a left-fold over conjunctions with the following attempted derivation from a right-fold implementation. We η-expand and unfold to a recursive help function like before.

```
(define (conj g . g*)
  (cond
    ((null? g*) g)
    (else (conj₂ g (apply conj g*)))))
= { η-expansion }
(define ((conj g . g*) s)
  (cond
    ((null? g*) (g s))
    (else ((conj₂ g (apply conj g*)) s))))
⊂
(define ((conj g . g*) s)
  (C g g* s))

(define (C g g* s)
  (cond
    ((null? g*) (g s))
    (else ((conj₂ g (apply conj g*)) s))))
```

In C, we can substitute in the definition of conj₂ and β-reduce. We once again η-expand the call to (apply conj g*) to substitute with the definition of conj and eliminate the apply. There, however, we get stuck.

```
(define (C g g* s)
  (cond
    ((null? g*) (g s))
    (else ((conj₂ g (apply conj g*)) s))))
= { by definition of conj₂ and β-reduction }
(define (C g g* s)
  (cond
    ((null? g*) (g s))
    (else
      (append-map∞
        (apply conj g*)
        (g s)))))
= { η-expand to use the definition of conj }
(define (C g g* s)
  (cond
    ((null? g*) (g s))
    (else
      (append-map∞
        (λ (s)
          (C (car g*) (cdr g*) s))
        (g s)))))
```

At this point in the left-fold derivation, these calls are accumulating in a stack-like discipline, so we can simplify and pass g and s together as a stream. The equivalent right-fold implementation, however, is in a kind of continuation-passing style for non-deterministic computations. Each goal in the list seems to require a closure for every recursive call. Building these closures is expensive. Similar behavior shows up in the right-fold variant of disj. Basic programming horse sense suggests the more elegant variants from Listing 3, and could partly explain the performance gap.

```
(C g (list g₁ g₂) s)
=
(append-map∞
  (λ (s)
    (C g₁ (list g₂) s))
  (g s))
=
(append-map∞
  (λ (s)
    (append-map∞
      (λ (s)
        (C g₂ '() s))
      (g₁ s)))
  (g s))
=
(append-map∞
  (λ (s)
    (append-map∞
      (λ (s)
        (g₂ s))
      (g₁ s)))
  (g s))
```

The new disj and conj functions are, we believe, sufficiently high-level for programmers in implementations without macros. Though this note mainly concerns working towards an internal macro-less kernel language, it may also have something to say about the miniKanren-level surface syntax, namely that even the miniKanren language could do without its conde syntax (a disjunction of conjunctions that looks superficially like Scheme's **cond**) and have the programmer use these new underlying logical primitives. In Listing 4, we implement carmelit-subway as an example, and it reads much better than the 11 binary logical operators the programmer would have needed in the earlier version.

```
(defrel (carmelit-subway a b c d e f)
  (disj
    (conj (== a 'carmel-center)
          (== b 'golomb)
          (== c 'masada)
          (== d 'haneviim)
          (== e 'hadar-city-hall)
          (== f 'downtown))
    (conj (== a 'downtown)
          (== b 'hadar-city-hall)
          (== c 'haneviim)
          (== d 'masada)
          (== e 'golomb)
          (== f 'carmel-center)))))
```

Listing 4. A new Carmelit subway without conde

```
(define-syntax conda
  (syntax-rules ()
    ((conda g) g)
    ((conda g₁ g₂) (conj g₁ g₂))
    ((conda g₁ g₂ g₃ g* ...)
     (ifte g₁ g₂ (conda g₃ g* ...)))))

(define (conda g . g*)
  (cond
    ((null? g*) g)
    ((null? (cdr g*)) (conj g (car g*)))
    (else
     (ifte g (car g*) (apply conda (cdr g*))))))
```

Listing 5. A re-implemented conda macro and its functional equivalent

4   Tidying Up the Impure Operators

The conda of *TRS2e* provides nested "if-then-else" behavior (the a is because at most one line succeeds). It relies on microKanren's underlying ifte. That conda requires one or more conjuncts per clause and one or more clauses. Once again, we would like to have an equivalently expressive feature without resorting to macros. Unlike the *TRS2e* implementation, the versions of conda in Listing 5 consume a sequence of goals. They consume those goals in "if-then" pairs, perhaps followed by a final "else"; we have no choice if we want to proceed without using a macro.

We defer the derivation of our new conda solution to the Appendix. Rather than building a largely redundant implementation of condu, we expose the higher-order goal once to the user. The programmer can simulate condu by wrapping once around every test goal. We do however take this opportunity to also lift the inner function loop to a top-level definition.

```
(define ((conda . g*) s)
  (cond
    ((null? g*) '())
    (else (A (cdr g*) ((car g*) s) s))))

(define (A g* s∞ s)
  (cond
    ((null? g*) s∞)
    ((null? (cdr g*)) (append-map∞ (car g*) s∞))
    (else (ifs∞te s∞ (car g*) (cdr g*) s))))

(define (ifs∞te s∞ g g+ s)
  (cond
    ((null? s∞) (A (cdr g+) ((car g+) s) s))
    ((pair? s∞) (append-map∞ g s∞))
    (else (λ () (ifs∞te (s∞) g g+ s)))))

(define ((once g) s)
  (O (g s)))

(define (O s∞)
  (cond
    ((null? s∞) '())
    ((pair? s∞) (cons (car s∞) '()))
    (else (λ () (O (s∞))))))
```

Listing 6. A functional conda, ifte, and once

5   Removing More Macros

The 2013 microKanren paper demonstrates how to implement a side-effect free macro-less Kanren language in an eager host. In Listing 7 we display these alternative mechanisms for introducing fresh logic variables, executing queries, and introducing delay and interleave. The versions in Listing 7 are slightly adjusted to be consistent with this presentation.

Each of these has drawbacks that compelled the *TRS2e* authors to instead use macro-based alternatives in the kernel layer. In this section, we explicitly address those drawbacks and point out some other non-macro alternatives that may demand more from a host language than the original microKanren choices, and make some recommendations.

```
(define ((call/fresh f) s)
  (let ((v (state->newvar s)))
    ((f v) (incr-var-ct s))))

(define (call/initial-state n g)
  (reify/1st
    (take∞ n (pull (g initial-state)))))

(define (((Zzz g) s))
  (g s))

> (call/initial-state 3
    (call/fresh
      (λ (x)
        (== x 'cat))))
```

Listing 7. Definition and use of functional microKanren equivalents of *TRS2e* kernel macros

5.1   Logic Variables

Many of the choices for these last options hinge on a representation of logic variables. Every implementation must have a mechanism to produce the next fresh logic variable. The choice of variable representation will affect the implementation of unification and constraint solving, the actual introduction of fresh variables, as well as answer projection, the formatting and presentation of a query's results. Depending on the implementation, the variables may also need additional functions to support them. In a shallow embedding, designing a set of logic variables means either using a **struct**-like mechanism to custom-build a datatype hidden from the microKanren programmer, or designating some subset of the host language's values for use as logic variables. Using **struct**s and limiting the visibility of the constructors and accessors is a nice option for languages that support it.

The choice of which host language values to take for logic variables divides roughly into the structurally equal and the referentially equal. For an example of the latter, consider representing each variable using a vector, and identifying vectors by their unique memory location. This latter approach models logic variables as a single global pool rather than reused separately across each disjunct, and so requires more logic variables overall. The microKanren approach uses natural numbers as an indexed set of variables, which necessitates removing numbers from the user's term language.

5.2   **fresh**

There are numerous ways to represent variables, and so too are there many ways to introduce fresh variables. In the microKanren approach, the current variable index is one of the fields of the state threaded through the computation; to go from index to variable is the identity function, and the state->newvar function we use can be just an accessor. The function `incr-var-ct` can reconstruct that state with the variable count incremented. The `call/fresh` function, shown in Listing 7, takes as its first argument a goal parameterized by the name of a fresh variable. `call/fresh` then applies that function with the newly created logic variable, thereby associating that host-language lexical variable with the DSL's logic variable. This lets the logic language "piggyback" on the host's lexical scoping and variable lookup, as shown in Listing 7.

This approach also means, however, that absent some additional machinery the user must introduce those new logic variables one at a time, once each per `call/fresh` expression, as though manually currying all functions in a functional language. This made programs larger than the relational `append` difficult to write and to read, and that amount of threading and re-threading state for each variable is costly. We could easily support, say instead, three variables at a time—force the user to provide a three-argument function and always supply three fresh variables at a time. Though practically workable the choice of some arbitrary quantity k of variables at a time, or choices k_1 and k_2 for that matter, seems unsatisfactory. It could make sense to inspect a procedure for its arity at runtime and introduce exactly that many variables, in languages that support that ability. In many languages, a procedure's arity is more complex than a single number. Variadic functions and keyword arguments all complicate the story of a procedure's arity. A form like **case-lambda** means that a single procedure may have several disjoint arities. The arity inspection approach could be a partial solution where the implementer restricts the programmer to using functions with fixed arity.

One last approach is to directly expose to the user a mechanism to create a new variable, and allow the programmer to use something like a **let** binding to do their own variable introduction and name binding. Under any referentially transparent representation of variables, this would mean that the programmer would be responsible for tracking the next lexical variable. This last approach pairs best with referentially opaque variables where the operation to produce a new variable allocates some formerly unused memory location so the programmer does not need to track the next logic variable. See sokuza-kanren [9] for an example of this style. With this latter approach, however, we can expose `var` directly to the programmer who can use **let** bindings to introduce several logic variables simultaneously.

5.3   run

Listing 7 also shows how we have implemented a run-like behavior without using macros. Using a referentially transparent implementation of logic variables, we can accomplish the job of `run` and `run*` by a `call/initial-state`-like function. The query is itself expressed as a goal that introduces the first logic variable q. A run-like operator displays the result with respect to the first variable introduced. This means pruning superfluous variables from the answer, producing a single value from the accumulated equations, and numbering the fresh variables. When logic variables are only identified by reference equality, the language implementation must pass the same *pointer-identical* logic variable into both the query and into the answer projection, called `reify`. The pointer-based logic variable approach forces the programmer to explicitly invoke `reify` as though it were a goal as the last step of executing the query, as in the first example in Listing 8, or create a special variable introduction mechanism for the first variable, scoped over both the query and the answer projection, as in the second example.

```
(call/initial-state 1
  (let ((q (var 'q)))
    (conj
      (let ((x (var 'x)))
        (== q x))
      (reify q))))

(define (call/initial-state n f)
  (let ((q (var 'q)))
    (map (reify q)
         (take∞ n ((f q) initial-state)))))
```

Listing 8. Several approaches to reifying variables in `call/initial-state`. Here `initial-state` is a representation of an initially empty set of equations

5.4 `define`

The microKanren programmer can use their host language's **define** feature to construct relations as host-language functions, and manually introduce the delays in relations using a help function like `Zzz` (Listing 7) to introduce delays, as in the original implementation. [6] This may be a larger concession than it looks, since it exposes the delay and interleave mechanism to the user, and both correct interleaving and, in an eager host language, even the termination of relation *definitions* rely on a whole-program correctness property of relation definitions having a delay. `Zzz` *if always used correctly* would be sufficient to address that problem, but forgetting it just once could cause the entire program to loop. Turning the delaying and interleaving into a user-level operation means giving the programmer some explicit control over the search, and that in turn could transform a logic language into an imperative one. Another downside of relying on a host-language **define** is that the programmer must now take extra care not to provide multiple goals in the body. The **define** form will treat all but the last expression as statements and silently drop them, rather than conjoin them as in `defrel`. For those implementing a shallowly embedded stream-based implementation in an eager host language, that can be a subtle mistake to debug.

6 Future Work

This note shows how to provide a somewhat more concise core language that significantly reduces the need for macros, and provides some alternatives for those working without macros that may be more practical than those of Hemann and Friedman [6].

Forcing ourselves to define `disj` and `conj` functionally, and with the restrictions we placed on ourselves in this re-implementation, removed a degree of implementation freedom and led us to what seems like the right solution. The result is closer to the design of Prolog, where the user represents conjunction of goals in the body of a clause with a comma and disjunction, either implicitly in listing various clauses or explicitly with a semicolon. The prior desugaring macros do not seem to suggest how to associate the calls to the binary primitives—both left and right look equally nice—where these transformations suggest a reason for the performance difference. The functional `conda` re-implementation is now also variadic, and exposing `once` to the programmer makes using committed choice almost as easy as with the earlier `condu`.

Existing techniques for implementing `defrel`, `fresh`, and `run` (and `run*`) without macros have serious drawbacks. They include exposing the implementation of streams and delays, and the inefficiency and clumsiness of introducing variables one at a time, or the need to reason about global state. With a few more runtime features from the host language, an implementer can overcome some of those drawbacks, and may find one of the suggested proposals an acceptable trade-off.

From time to time we find that the usual miniKanren implementation is *itself* lower-level than we would like to program with relations. Early microKanren implementations restrict themselves to **syntax-rules** macros. Some programmers use macros to extend the language further as with `matche` [8]. Some constructions over miniKanren, such as `minikanren-ee` [1], may rely on more expressive macro systems like `syntax-parse` [2].

We would still like to know if our desiderata here are *causally* related to good miniKanren performance. Can we reason at the implementation level and peer through to the implications for performance? If left associating `conj` is indeed uniformly a dramatic improvement, the community might consider reclassifying left-associative conjunction as a matter of correctness rather than an optimization, as in "tail call optimization" vs. "Properly Implemented Tail Call Handling" [3]. Regardless, we hope this document narrows the gap between macro-free microKanrens and those using macro systems, and leads to more elegant, expressive and efficient implementations regardless of functional host language.

Acknowledgments

Thanks to Michael Ballantyne, Greg Rosenblatt, Ken Shan, and Jeremy Siek for their helpful discussions and ideas. Our thanks to Yafei Yang and Darshal Shetty for their implementation suggestions. We would also like to thank our anonymous reviewers for their insightful contributions.

Appendix

A `conj` Derivation

Starting with the variadic function based on the macro in Listing 2, we first η-expand and split the definition.

```
(define (conj g . g*)
  (cond
    ((null? g*) g)
    (else
     (apply conj
       (cons (conj₂ g (car g*)) (cdr g*))))))
= { η-expansion }
(define ((conj g . g*) s)
  (cond
    ((null? g*) (g s))
    (else
     ((apply conj
        (cons (conj₂ g (car g*)) (cdr g*))) s))))
⊂
(define ((conj g . g*) s)
  (C g g* s))

(define (C g g* s)
  (cond
    ((null? g*) (g s))
    (else
     ((apply conj
        (cons (conj₂ g (car g*)) (cdr g*)))
      s))))
```

We next substitute for the definitions of conj and conj₂.

```
(define (C g g* s)
  (cond
    ((null? g*) (g s))
    (else
     ((apply conj
        (cons (conj₂ g (car g*)) (cdr g*)))
      s))))
= { by the definition of conj }
(define (C g g* s)
  (cond
    ((null? g*) (g s))
    (else
     (C (conj₂ g (car g*)) (cdr g*) s))))
= { by the definition of conj₂ }
(define (C g g* s)
  (cond
    ((null? g*) (g s))
    (else
     (C (λ (s)
          (append-map∞ (car g*) (g s)))
        (cdr g*)
        s))))
```

This definition of C sequences the invocations of goal and state in the order they appear. append-map∞ acts like a non-deterministic compose operator. In each recursive call, we accumulate by mapping, using append-map∞'s special delaying implementation of Kanren-language streams, the next goal in the list.

```
(C g (list g₁ g₂) s)
=
(C (λ (s)
      (append-map∞ g₁
        (g s)))
   (list g₂)
   s)
=
(C (λ (s)
      (append-map∞ g₂
        ((λ (s)
           (append-map∞ g₁
             (g s)))
         s)))
   '()
   s)
=
((λ (s)
    (append-map∞ g₂
      ((λ (s)
         (append-map∞ g₁
           (g s)))
       s)))
 s)
```

The state does not change in the recursion: C only needs s to *build* the stream. Therefore we can assemble the stream on the way in—instead of passing in g and s separately, we pass in their combination as a stream. The function is tail recursive; we can change the signature in the one and only external call and the recursive call. Adding the trivial base case to conj, yields the version shown in Listing 3.

B   conda Derivation

```
(define (conda g . g*)
  (cond
    ((null? g*) g)
    ((null? (cdr g*)) (conj g (car g*)))
    (else
     (ifte g (car g*) (apply conda (cdr g*))))))
= { η-expansion }
(define ((conda g . g*) s)
  (cond
    ((null? g*) (g s))
```

```
    ((null? (cdr g*)) ((conj g (car g*)) s))
    (else
      ((ifte g (car g*) (apply conda (cdr g*)))
       s))))
c
(define ((conda g . g*) s)
  (A g g* s))
(define (A g g* s)
  (cond
    ((null? g*) (g s))
    ((null? (cdr g*)) ((conj g (car g*)) s))
    (else
      ((ifte g (car g*) (apply conda (cdr g*)))
       s))))
= { let bindings and η-expansion }
(define (A g g* s)
  (cond
    ((null? g*) (g s))
    (else
      (let ((g1 (car g*)) (g* (cdr g*)))
        (cond
          ((null? g*) ((conj g g1) s))
          (else
            ((ifte g g1
               (λ (s)
                 ((apply conda g*) s)))
             s)))))))
= { by definition of conda, conj, and C }
(define (A g g* s)
  (cond
    ((null? g*) (g s))
    (else
      (let ((g1 (car g*)) (g* (cdr g*)))
        (cond
          ((null? g*) (append-map∞ g1 (g s)))
          (else
            ((ifte g g1
               (λ (s)
                 (A (car g*) (cdr g*) s)))
             s)))))))
= { by definition of ifte and a β reduction }
(define (A g g* s)
  (cond
    ((null? g*) (g s))
    (else
```

```
(let ((g1 (car g*)) (g* (cdr g*)))
  (cond
    ((null? g*) (append-map∞ g1 (g s)))
    (else
     (let loop ((s∞ (g s)))
       (cond
         ((null? s∞) (A (car g*) (cdr g*) s))
         ((pair? s∞) (append-map∞ g1 s∞))
         (else (λ () (loop (s∞)))))))))))))))))
```

At this point g and s in conda are *begging* to be passed as a stream s∞; we oblige them. We lift that local function loop to a global definition, passing all the parameters it needs. Since the only call to ifs∞te is in A, we know that ifs∞te's third parameter will always be a non-empty list.

```
(define (A g* s∞)
  (cond
    ((null? g*) s∞)
    (else
     (let ((g1 (car g*)) (g* (cdr g*)))
       (cond
         ((null? g*) (append-map∞ g1 s∞))
         (else
          (let loop ((s∞ s∞))
            (cond
              ((null? s∞) (A (cdr g*) ((car g*) s)))
              ((pair? s∞) (append-map∞ g1 s∞))
              (else (λ () (loop (s∞)))))))))))))
⊂
(define (A g* s∞)
  (cond
    ((null? g*) s∞)
    (else
     (let ((g1 (car g*)) (g* (cdr g*)))
       (cond
         ((null? g*) (append-map∞ g1 s∞))
         (else (ifs∞te s∞ g1 g* s))))))))

(define (ifs∞te s∞ g g+ s)
  (cond
    ((null? s∞) (A (cdr g+) ((car g+) s)))
    ((pair? s∞) (append-map∞ g s∞))
    (else (λ () (ifs∞te (s∞) g g+ s)))))
```

If we also add a line in conda to dispatch with the trivial case, we arrive at the definition in Listing 6. Most of Listing 6 is a functional implementation of that cascade behavior. A knows it has at least one goal; it's job is to determine if there is precisely one goal, precisely two goals, or more than two goals.

References

[1] Ballantyne, M., King, A., Felleisen, M.: Macros for domain-specific languages. In: Proceedings of the ACM on Programming Languages 4.OOPSLA, pp. 1–29 (2020)
[2] Culpepper, R.: Fortifying macros. J. Funct. Prog. **22**(4–5), 439–476 (2012)
[3] Felleisen, M.: Re: Question about tail recursion (2014). https://lists.racket-lang.org/users/archive/2014-August/063844.html
[4] Friedman, D.P., et al.: The Reasoned Schemer, 2nd edn. The MIT Press (2018). ISBN:0-262-53551-3. mitpress.mit.edu/books/reasoned-schemer-0
[5] Griswold, R.E., Griswold, M.T.: The Icon Programming Language, vol. 55. Prentice-Hall, Englewood Cliffs (1983)
[6] Hemann, J., Friedman, D.P.: μkanren: a minimal functional core for relational programming. In: Scheme 13 (2013). http://schemeworkshop.org/2013/papers/HemannMuKanren2013.pdf
[7] Hemann, J., et al.: A small embedding of logic programming with a simple complete search. In: Proceedings of DLS 2016. ACM (2016). https://doi.org/10.1145/2989225.2989230
[8] Keep, A.W., et al.: A pattern matcher for miniKanren or How to get into trouble with CPS macros. In: Technical Report CPSLO-CSC-09-03, p. 37 (2009)
[9] Kiselyov, O.: The Taste of Logic Programming (2006). http://okmij.org/ftp/Scheme/misc.html#sokuzakanren
[10] Rosenblatt, G., et al.: First-order miniKanren representation: great for tooling and search. In: Proceedings of the miniKanren Workshop, p. 16 (2019)

Alternative Methods for Retaining Explicit and Finding Implicit Sharing in Embedded DSLs

Curtis D'Alves[✉], Lucas Dutton, Steven Gonder,
and Christopher Kumar Anand

McMaster University, 1280 Main St W, Hamilton, Canada
curtis.dalves@gmail.com

Abstract. Detection of sharing is a known challenge for implementers of embedded domain specific languages (DSLs). There are many solutions, each with their advantages and drawbacks. Many solutions are based on observable sharing, that requires either a monadic interface or use of unsafe referencing, e.g., Data.Reify. Monadic interfaces are considered unsuitable for domain experts, and the use of unsafe referencing leads to fragile software.

Kiselyov's methods for implicit and explicit sharing detection for finally tagless style DSLs is an elegant solution without having to resort to unsafe observable sharing. However these methods are not applicable to all types of DSLs (including those generating hypergraphs). We will present alternative methods which handle these cases. The main difference comes from the use of a trie to perform hash-consing. Our method for implicit sharing essentially trades worst-case exponential growth in computation for increased memory footprint. To mitigate this issue, our method for explicit sharing reduces the memory footprint.

Keywords: DSL · sharing · common-subexpression elimination · Haskell

1 Introduction

Embedded DSL's have proven useful for many applications, and there are multiple ways of doing the embedding. Domain experts are more comfortable with embeddings presented as a collection of pure functions. On the other hand, optimizing code generators and other downstream uses would be much easier to implement in the context of a monad. In particular code graph generation outside of a monad does not benefit from observable sharing in Haskell. Kiselyov [7] solves this problem by presenting a method for implementing eDSLs in finally tagless form that generates a directed acyclic graph (DAG) with sharing. However, as we will explain in Sects. 2.3 and 2.4, for DSL functions that return multiple outputs (e.g., tuples, lists, etc.), Kiselyov's method of implicitly detecting sharing may require computation exponential in the size of the program, and his method of explicitly declaring sharing is inapplicable.

S. Chang (Ed.): TFP 2023, LNCS 13868, pp. 92–105, 2023.
https://doi.org/10.1007/978-3-031-38938-2_6

In the toy example

```
class Exp repr where
  variable :: String -> repr Int
  constant :: String -> repr Int
  add :: repr Int -> repr Int -> repr Int
  novel :: (repr Int,repr Int) -> (repr Int,repr Int)
```

the function novel will exhibit this issue. Since it returns multiple outputs via a native tuple or list, it will cause duplication of computation that cannot be captured by Kiselyov's explicit sharing method. We will illustrate this implementation issue in Sect. 2.4. Encountering this issue in our own work with eDSLs for code generation caused a computational explosion on large DAGs.

In this paper, we review Kiselyov's methods, identifying the core issue, and present methods for implementing embedded DSLs with sharing that avoid unsafe referencing (i.e., unsafePerformIO) [5], maintain all the benefits of being embedded in the Haskell ecosystem and are computationally feasible. This means DSL functions are pure, type-safe and can return Haskell container types (i.e., tuples, lists, etc.) without breaking sharing. All code will be hosted at https:// github.com/dalvescb/AltSharingInEDSL_Paper

2   Background: Detecting Sharing

Consider the naive DSL implemented as a Haskell data type:

```
data Exp
  = Add Exp Exp
  | Variable String
  | Constant Int
```

Expressions generate Abstract Syntax Trees (ASTs), but consider this example,

```
v0 = Variable "v0"
exp0 = Add v0 (Constant 0)
exp1 = Add exp0 exp0
```

in which the expression exp0 is shared, and will therefore be stored once in memory. For large expressions with lots of sharing, this can make a substantial difference.

One of the first things the developer will do is write a pretty printer. That recursive function will traverse the data structure as a tree, and pretty print exp0 twice. This inefficiency is a real problem for code generation, and naive traversal of the AST does the opposite of the common-subexpression elimination performed by a good optimizing compiler. To avoid this, rather than representing the code as an AST, we should use a DAG, retaining all of the sharing in the original DSL code.

One way of maintaining sharing is by observable sharing (see Sect. 3 in [7]). In Haskell, this requires a monadic interface. Monads are useful, but don't match the expectations of domain experts [8].

2.1   Finally Tagless DSLs

It would be nice to make use of monadic state when we need it (i.e., for converting to a DAG) while hiding it behind a nice pure interface. The finally tagless approach [1] is popular for accomplishing this. In this approach, DSL expressions are built using type-class methods that wrap the DSL in a parameterized representation. For example, the previous data-type-based DSL could be written in finally tagless style as

```
class Exp repr where
  add :: repr Int -> repr Int -> repr Int
  variable :: String -> repr Int
  constant :: Int -> repr Int
```

We can then create different instances to implement different functionality. For example, we can implement a pretty printer

```
newtype Pretty a = Pretty { runPretty :: String }

instance Exp Pretty where
  add x y = Pretty $ "("++runPretty x++") + ("++runPretty y++")"
  variable x = Pretty x
  constant x = Pretty $ show x
```

Or generate an AST

```
newtype AST a = AST { genAST :: Exp }

instance Exp AST where
  add x y =  AST $ Add (genAST x) (genAST y)
  variable x = AST $ Variable x
  constant x = AST $ Constant x
```

Finally tagless style provides extensible, user friendly DSLs. By providing one interface for a variety of functionality, you can choose between shallow and deep embeddings (see [6] and [9]) and can easily extend the DSL without having to alter the original class definition.

2.2   Implicit Sharing via Hash-Consing

The goal of detecting sharing is to generate a graph structure (like the AST in Sect. 2) but with sharing of common subexpressions. So we're going to generate a Directed Acyclic Graph (DAG) instead of an AST. For example, we can use the following DAG structure that explicitly references nodes by a unique identifier

```
type NodeID = Int
data Node = NAdd NodeID NodeID
```

```
                | NVariable String
                | NConstant Int

newtype DAG = DAG (BiMap Node) deriving Show
```

Kiselyov's method for detecting implicit sharing in finally tagless style uses hash-consing [7]. Hash-consing is based on a bijection of nodes and a set of identifiers, e.g.,

```
data BiMap a -- abstract
lookup_key :: Ord a => a -> BiMap a -> Maybe Int
lookup_val :: Int -> BiMap a -> a
insert :: Ord a => a -> BiMap a -> (Int,BiMap a)
empty :: BiMap a
```

The method can be performed using any data structure that provides the above interface. An efficient implementation would use hashing and linear probing, as is done by Thai in his Master's thesis [10].

In order to generate such a data structure, we will need to keep track of the current maximum identifier to keep them unique. The representation for the finally tagless instance is then a wrapper around a state monad that holds the DAG being constructed in its state and returns the current (top) NodeID:

```
newtype Graph a = Graph { unGraph :: State DAG NodeID }

instance Exp Graph where
  constant x = Graph (hashcons $ NConstant x)
  variable x = Graph (hashcons $ NVariable x)
  add e1 e2 = Graph (do
                    h1 <- unGraph e1
                    h2 <- unGraph e2
                    hashcons $ NAdd h1 h2)
```

The trick to uncovering sharing is in the hashcons function, which inserts a new node into the current DAG, but not before checking if it is already there.

```
hashcons :: Node -> State DAG NodeID
hashcons e = do
  DAG m <- get
  case lookup_key e m of
    Nothing -> let (k,m') = insert e m
               in put (DAG m') >> return k
    Just k -> return k
```

The technique is essentially that of hash-consing, popularized by its use in LISP compilers, but discovered by Ershov in 1958 [3]. Other works have explored the use of type-safe hash-consing in embedded DSLs, see [4].

2.3   Limitations of Hash-Consing

When we wrap our state monad in finally tagless style, we lose some expected sharing. In the following code, the use of the let causes the computation $x + y$ to only occur once

```
haskellSharing x y =
 let
    z = x + y
 in z + z
```

Implicit sharing via hash-consing prevents duplication in the resulting DAG, but unfortunately doesn't prevent redundant computation. Consider the following equivalent attempt at using Haskell's built-in sharing in the finally tagless DSL

```
dslSharing :: Exp Graph -> Exp Graph -> Exp Graph
dslSharing x y =
   let
      z = add x y
   in add z z
```

Knowing that z is a wrapper around a state monad, and recalling the implementation of add via hash-consing above, the values h1 and h2 are separately evaluated through the state monad, even if e1 and e2 are the same shared Haskell value. Hash-consing will prevent these redundancies from appearing in the resulting DAG, but in the process of discovering the sharing, the entire unshared AST will still be traversed.

Consider a chain of adds with sharing, for example

```
addChains :: Exp repr => Expr Int -> Expr Int
addChains x0 =
   let
      x1 = add x0 x0
      x2 = add x1 x1
      . . .
   in xn
```

As shown in Fig. 1, this code will perform approximately 2^{n+1} hashcons operations, where n is the number of adds.

2.4   Explicit Sharing and Limitations

Kiselyov [7] recognized that the amount of computation with hash-consing "may take a long time for large programs," and proposed an ad-hoc solution, explicit sharing via a custom let construct

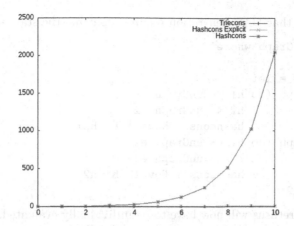

Fig. 1. Number of calls to **hashcons** plotted against the number of **add** operations performed. Hash-consing is performed without explicit sharing and is clearly exponential, Triecons (without explicit sharing) and Hashcons Explicit (with explicit sharing) overlap and are both linear.

```
class ExpLet repr where
    let_ :: repr a -> (repr a -> repr b) -> repr b
instance ExpLet Graph where
    let_ e f = Graph (do x <- unGraph e
                         unGraph $ f (Graph (return x)))
```

which can be used to rewrite **addChains** as

```
addChains x =
  let_ x (\x0 ->
  let_ (add x0 x0)  (\x1 ->
  let_ (add x1 x1)  (\x2 ->
  ...
  )))
```

This makes the code a bit clunky and adds an extra burden on the DSL writer, but it prevents unnecessary hash-consing in our example.

However the method does not work for DSL functions returning multiple outputs via tuples or container types like lists. Generating a hypergraph or bipartite graph structure that allows operation nodes like **add** to have edges to multiple outputs is one way this problem will arise. For example, in our own research we implemented a DSL for an instruction set architecture that generates a bipartite graph of instructions and the registers they act upon. Attempting to generate a graph where an instruction outputs multiple values will result in returning multiple independent state monads.

We can concisely illustrate this problem by adding the following instruction to our DSL that attempts to return two separate nodes in the DAG at once

```
novel :: (repr Int,repr Int) -> (repr Int,repr Int)
```

The issue is that DAG generation requires splitting the state monad in two:

```
instance Exp Graph where
  ...
  novel e1 e2 = let
    g1 = Graph (do h1 <- unGraph e1
                   h2 <- unGraph e2
                   hashcons $ Novel1 h1 h2)
    g2 = Graph (do h1 <- unGraph e1
                   h2 <- unGraph e2
                   hashcons $ Novel2 h1 h2)
    in (g1,g2)
```

Each output it returns will now have to be individually evaluated, so a chain of DSL functions that output 2 or more values will suffer from the same exponential explosion of hash-consing operations, and trying to adapt the let construct above, just creates another function with the same problem (multiple outputs).

One solution to this issue is to integrate container types such as tuples and lists into the DSL language. However doing this eliminates the advantage of having an embedded language. Manipulating tuple values will be cumbersome, constantly requiring calls to custom implementations of `fst`, `snd` etc. And for lists you'll lose access to built-in Haskell list functionality. To get the full advantage of embedding a DSL it should not only inherit the host language's syntactic and semantic structure, but also it's programming environment, as is argued in [2].

3   Implicit Sharing via Byte String ASTs

The heart of our problem is that whenever we need to sequence the state of the inputs for one of our DSL functions we want to first check if it's already been evaluated. But how do we do that without first evaluating it to gain access to its unique identifier? We need some way to uniquely identify it outside the monad.

Our proposed solution is to build a serialized AST using byte strings for each node along with our DAG. The byte string stays outside the monad, while the DAG remains inside. We can do this efficiently by replacing the `BiMap` with a trie. In our toy example, we use the package `bytestring-trie`.

```
data Graph a = Graph { unGraph :: State DAG NodeID
                     , stringAST :: ByteString }

data DAG = DAG { unTrie :: Trie (Node,NodeID)
               , maxID  :: NodeID
               } deriving Show
```

This looks a bit different because the `BiMap` was a bijective relation between nodes and node ids, whereas the trie maps byte strings to pairs (node,node id). The DAG is expressed as a relation, by projecting out the values of the trie.

To prevent confusion, we name the hash-consing function in our method `triecons`:

```
triecons :: ByteString -> Node -> State DAG NodeID
triecons sAST node = do
  DAG trie maxID <- get
  case Trie.lookup sAST trie of
    Nothing -> let maxID' = maxID+1
                   trie' = Trie.insert sAST (node,maxID') trie
               in do put $ DAG trie' maxID'
                     return maxID'
    Just (_,nodeID) -> return nodeID
```

We use it to implement the DAG-building instance of the DSL, which looks a lot like the previous instance. The substantial differences are the `buildStringAST` calls which you can think of as pretty printing, but optimized for the trie, and the use of `seqArgs` (explained below):

```
instance Exp Graph where
  constant x = let
    node = NConstant x
    sAST = buildStringAST node []
    in Graph (triecons sAST $ NConstant x) sAST
  variable x = let
    node = NVariable x
    sAST = buildStringAST node []
    in Graph (triecons sAST $ NVariable x) sAST
  add e1 e2 = let
      sAST = buildStringAST "nadd" [e1,e2]
      sT = do ns <- seqArgs [e1,e2]
              case ns of
                [n1,n2] -> triecons sAST $ NAdd n1 n2
                _ -> error "black magic"
    in Graph sT sAST
```

The magic is in `seqArgs`. We only evaluate the inner state `sT` of each argument if we fail to find its corresponding serialized AST in the Trie.

```
seqArgs :: [Graph a] -> State DAG [NodeID]
seqArgs inps =
  let
    seqArg (Graph sT sAST) =
      do DAG trie _ <- get
         case Trie.lookup sAST  trie of
           Nothing -> sT
           Just (_,nodeID) -> return nodeID
  in sequence $ map seqArg inps
```

This will prevent redundant hash-consing without the need for explicit sharing, but at the expense of storing redundant byte strings.

3.1   Memory Limitations

The byte string AST being built will itself suffer from lack of sharing. We're essentially trading extra computation for extra memory. In our `addChains` example from Sect. 2.3, our method now has exponential scaling in memory instead of computation. This can be a good tradeoff, since memory is so plentiful in modern hardware, but still presents an issue.

4   Explicit Sharing of ByteString ASTs

We propose another solution to this issue, taking inspiration again from Kiselyov [7], by introducing an explicit construct for specifying sharing. This time, the construct will substitute the current byte string for a more compact label.

```
class Substitute repr where
   subT :: ByteString -> repr a -> repr a
instance Substitute Graph where
   subT s' (Graph g s _) = Graph g s' (Just s)

exampleSubT x y = let
  z = subT "z" (add x y)
  in add z z
```

For safety purposes, we need to keep track of a table of these labels and their corresponding ASTs, to make sure we don't use the same label for different serialized ASTs.

```
data DAG = DAG { dagTrie :: Trie (Node,NodeID)
                , dagSubMap :: Map ByteString ByteString
                , dagMaxID :: Int
                } deriving Show

data Graph a = Graph { unGraph :: State DAG NodeID
                     , unStringAST :: ByteString
                     , unSubT :: Maybe ByteString }
```

When a substitution is made via `subT`, the `unStringAST` field is replaced with the new label, and the previous serialized AST is placed in `unSubT`. When a `Graph` value is processed, the `unSubT` field is checked to see if it contains a label

```
seqArgs :: [Graph a] -> State DAG [NodeID]
seqArgs inps =
  let
    seqArg (Graph sT sAST mSubt) =
      do DAG trie _ _ <- get
         let sAST' = case mSubt of
```

```
                    Just s -> s
                    Nothing -> sAST
        case Trie.lookup sAST' trie of
          Nothing -> sT -- error "missing ast"
          Just (node,nodeID) ->
              do subTInsert mSubt sAST (node,nodeID)
                 return nodeID
   in sequence $ map seqArg inps
```

If the unSubT field contains a label, that means the current unStringAST field is a substitution that needs to be inserted into dagSubMap. The function subTInsert handles this

```
subTInsert :: Maybe ByteString -> ByteString
           -> (Node, NodeID) -> State DAG ()
subTInsert Nothing _ _ = return ()
subTInsert (Just s) sAST nodeID =
  do DAG trie subtMap _ <- get
     case Map.lookup sAST subtMap of
        Just sAST' -> if sAST == sAST'
                       then return ()
                       else error "tried to resubT"
        Nothing -> let cMap' = Map.insert sAST s subtMap
                       trie' = Trie.insert sAST nodeID trie
                   in modify (\dag -> dag { dagTrie = trie'
                                          , dagSubMap = cMap' })
```

We need to make sure we don't attempt to insert the same substitution for two different ASTs. Unfortunately, if there is a collision there's no way to escape the state monad to prevent or modify the substitution. In the toy example, compilation crashes, but we could catch an exception instead if we used the ExceptT transformer instead of a simple state monad. Either way it's up to the DSL user to ensure they don't reuse the same label as a substitution.

5   BenchMarking

Even with explicit sharing via substitutions, our method contains a reasonable amount of overhead in order to overcome the limitations of Kiselyov's method. The addChains example altered for explicit sharing with both methods presents a worst case scenario in terms of overhead comparison. Kiselyov's method is able to fully utilize its explicit sharing and our method requires many substitution lookups.

Table 1. Benchmarks of `addChains` example with full explicit sharing.

Size	150	200	10000	50000
Hash-Cons time	0.0 s	0.0 s	0.01 s	0.03 s
Hash-Cons alloc	619,296 bytes	739,304 bytes	28,662,592 bytes	155,993,544 bytes
Trie-Cons time	0.0 s	0.0 s	0.03 s	0.16 s
Trie-Cons alloc	1,773,416 bytes	2,333,680 bytes	129,146,808 bytes	723,437,504 bytes

Table 1 gives a set of benchmarks comparing our method with Kiselyov's, both taking full advantage of explicit sharing. It's clear Kiselyov's method performs better in this situation, however it should be noted our method is still viable for solving very large DAG's in reasonable amounts of time/memory.

For more interesting benchmarks, we need to consider a more sophisticated DSL. We defined a DSL for an instruction set architecture as mentioned in Sect. 2.4. It will has the following interface

```
class ISA repr where
    -- | Load from memory into a GPR
    ldMR :: repr MR -> Int -> (repr GPR, repr MR)
    -- | Store a GPR into memory
    stdMR    :: repr MR -> Int -> repr GPR -> repr MR
    -- | Bitwise NAND of two 64-bit general-purpose registers (NNGRK)
    nandG    :: repr GPR -> repr GPR -> repr GPR
    -- | Bitwise NOR of two 64-bit general-purpose registers (NOGRK)
    norG     :: repr GPR -> repr GPR -> repr GPR
    -- | Bitwise NXOR of two 64-bit general-purpose registers (NXGRK)
    eqvG     :: repr GPR -> repr GPR -> repr GPR
    -- | Addition of two 64-bit general-purpose registers (AGRK)
    addG     :: repr GPR -> repr GPR -> repr GPR
    ...
```

This language can be used to encode basic blocks of assembly code. These basic blocks may return multiple outputs, preventing us from using explicit sharing via let constructs. For example,

```
add2 :: ISA repr => (repr GPR, repr GPR) -> (repr GPR, repr GPR)
add2 (a, b) =
    let
        a' = addG a b
        b' = addG a' b
    in (a', b')
```

We used this language to implement approximations of vector `cos` and `tan` (i.e., a loop body that cos or tan over an input array). The loop body was unrolled by a factor of four resuling in a large DAG.

We profiled `cos` using both Kiselyov's method (i.e., hash-consing) and our own (i.e., trie-consing with some explicit sharing). It wasn't possible to use Kiselyov's explicit sharing method in this case so our code was able to achieve greater performance, 154% speedup, with only a small increase in memory consumption (see Fig. 2).

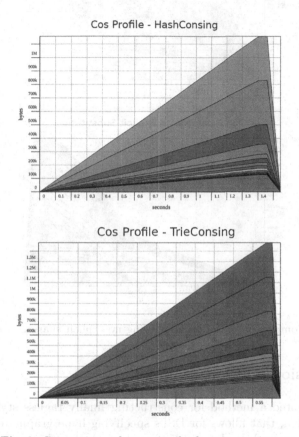

Fig. 2. Comparison of cos using hash-cons vs trie-cons.

For `tan`, we were unable to generate a resulting code graph using Kiselyov's method. Using explicit sharing via let constructs wasn't possible due to the multiple outputs issue and without it the amount of computation due to redundant hash-consing was simply too large, and would not terminate.

We were able to generate `tan` using our method both without and with our explicit sharing, however without explicit sharing we consumed an unreasonable amount of memory (see Fig. 3). It should be noted, the main source of redundant computation in `tan` is the reuse of computed values of `cos` and `sin`. By simply explicitly sharing just those values we achieved the significant speedup shown in Fig. 3.

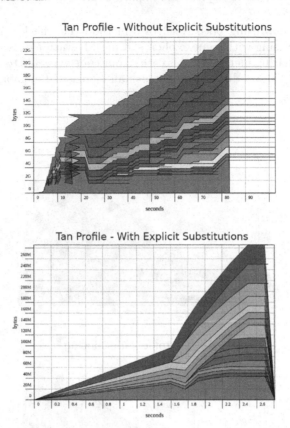

Fig. 3. Comparison of tan profiling using no explicit sharing vs explicit.

6   Conclusion and Future Work

We have presented a method for constructing finally tagless style DSLs with sharing detection, that allows for DSLs specifying hypergraphs (e.g., functions with multiple outputs). It also avoids the use of unsafe referencing as performed when doing observable sharing, c.f. [5].

The method has its drawbacks in terms of memory usage, but these can be mitigated by explicitly specifying sharing. This does present an extra burden on the DSL writer to implement explicit sharing when necessary and ensure labels are not reused. Future work may investigate the use of a preprocessor or plugin to automate explicit sharing. Unlike an explicit let construct, it would be fairly straightforward to automatically bind subT operations to any DSL function call.

Acknowledgements. We thank NSERC and IBM Canada Advanced Studies for supporting this work.

References

1. Carette, J., Kiselyov, O., Shan, C.: Finally tagless, partially evaluated. In: Shao, Z. (ed.) APLAS 2007. LNCS, vol. 4807, pp. 222–238. Springer, Heidelberg (2007). https://doi.org/10.1007/978-3-540-76637-7_15
2. Clements, J., Graunke, P., Krishnamurthi, S., Felleisen, M.: Little languages and their programming environments. In: Proceedings of the Monterey Workshop on Engineering Automation for Software Intensive System Integration, p. 1 (2001)
3. Ershov, A.P.: On programming of arithmetic operations. Commun. ACM **1**(8), 3–6 (1958)
4. Filliâtre, J.C., Conchon, S.: Type-safe modular hash-consing. In: Proceedings of the 2006 Workshop on ML, pp. 12–19 (2006)
5. Gill, A.: Type-safe observable sharing in Haskell. In: Proceedings of the 2nd ACM SIGPLAN Symposium on Haskell, pp. 117–128 (2009)
6. Jovanovic, V., Shaikhha, A., Stucki, S., Nikolaev, V., Koch, C., Odersky, M.: Yin-yang: concealing the deep embedding of dsls. In: Proceedings of the 2014 International Conference on Generative Programming: Concepts and Experiences, pp. 73–82 (2014)
7. Kiselyov, O.: Implementing explicit and finding implicit sharing in embedded DSLs. arXiv preprint arXiv:1109.0784 (2011)
8. O'Donnell, J.T.: Embedding a hardware description language in template haskell. In: Lengauer, C., Batory, D., Consel, C., Odersky, M. (eds.) Domain-Specific Program Generation. LNCS, vol. 3016, pp. 143–164. Springer, Heidelberg (2004). https://doi.org/10.1007/978-3-540-25935-0_9
9. Svenningsson, J., Axelsson, E.: Combining deep and shallow embedding for EDSL. In: Loidl, H.-W., Peña, R. (eds.) TFP 2012. LNCS, vol. 7829, pp. 21–36. Springer, Heidelberg (2013). https://doi.org/10.1007/978-3-642-40447-4_2
10. Thai, N.: Type-Safe Modeling for Optimization. Master's thesis, McMaster (2021)

Author Index

© The Editor(s) (if applicable) and The Author(s), under exclusive license
to Springer Nature Switzerland AG 2023
S. Chang (Ed.): TFP 2023, LNCS 13868, p. 107, 2023.
https://doi.org/10.1007/978-3-031-38938-2

Printed in the United States
by Baker & Taylor Publisher Services